Dedication: To my mother, Mabel M.,
and my Father, Elmer H. Kroepel:
music was a happiness in our home.
Bob Kroepel

WITHDRAWN

The **Deluxe Encyclopedia of Piano Chords** is a complete and thorough analysis of chords as applied to the piano keyboard. This study encompasses chord construction, usage, scales and rhythm patterns.

It is hoped that this text will enable the pianist or organist to effectively use and apply the full diversity of chord possibilities in creating interesting, personal and colorful musical styles.

Table of Contents

Here is a keyboard diagram showing the white keys of the piano keyboard and their location on the Grand Staff:

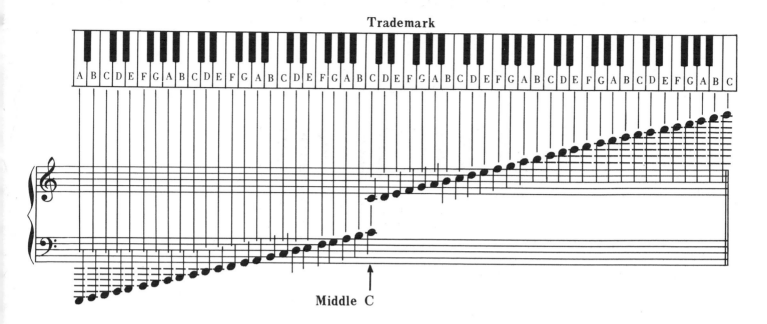

Notice that the number of leger lines needed to locate the pitches of the piano on the Grand Staff increase towards the ends of the keyboard.

To make it easier to read music is often written with the symbol **8va** instead of the exact number of leger lines.

8va means "octave." "Octave" comes from the Latin word "octava," meaning "eighth." An octave is the same letter eight letters to the left or right of the original:

A B C D E F G A B C D E F G A B C D E F G A B C ....
octave   original   octave

8va written above a note means to play the note with the same letter name an octave higher:

8va a basso means to play the note with the same letter name an octave lower:

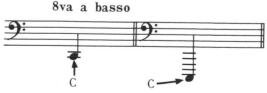

2 8va means two octaves higher: **2 8va a basso** means two octaves lower.

In music an **interval** is defined as the distance (in terms of pitch) between two notes.

The smallest interval on the piano keyboard is the **half-step:** a half-step is defined as the interval between two adjoining notes:

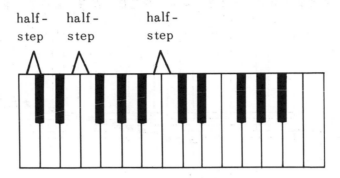

Two half-steps equal one **whole-step:**

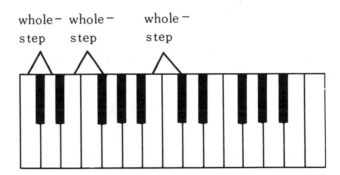

Musical symbols which alter the letter names of notes are called **accidentals.**

Here is a chart which explains the symbols used for accidentals:

Symbol	Name	Function	Example
♯	**Sharp**	raises pitch a half-step	
♭	**Flat**	lowers pitch a half-step	
𝄪	**Double-Sharp**	raises pitch two half-steps, or one whole-step	
♭♭	**Double-Flat**	lowers pitch two half-steps or one whole-step	
♮	**Natural**	cancels a sharp or a flat	

Major Scales.

The musical alphabet is a continuum, repeating endlessly the first seven letters of the English language alphabet:

A   B   C   D   E   F   G   A   B   C   D   E   F   G   A   B   C   D   E   F   G   A   ......etc.

A **scale** is a series of tones in an organized sequence.

A **major scale** is an eight-letter sequence of the musical alphabet.

The first letter of the major scale is called the **tonic note,** or **keynote:** the last letter of the major scale is the same as the keynote but is called the **octave.**

Ex. C major scale

```
C       D       E       F       G       A       B       C
|                                                       |
Keynote                                               Octave
```

The tones of the major scale can be numbered:

```
C       D       E       F       G       A       B       C
1.      2.      3.      4.      5.      6.      7.      8.
```

The numbers referring to the tones of a major scale are called **scale degrees.**

The musical relationships between the tones of a major scale can be expressed by means of **whole-steps** (abbreviated W) and **half-steps** (abbreviated H):

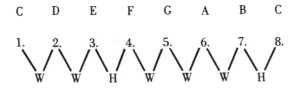

Here is the C major scale shown on a keyboard diagram:

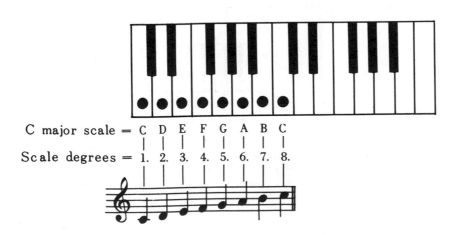

To preserve the whole-step and half-step relationships between the tones of a major scale the **key signature** indicates which notes are sharped or flatted.

Ex. The G major scale

The F sharp (F♯) in the key signature indicates
that this note is to be played F sharp (F♯)

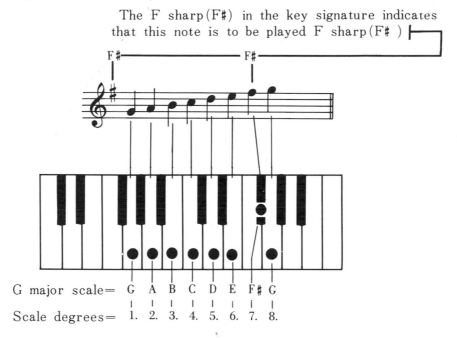

G major scale= G A B C D E F♯ G
Scale degrees= 1. 2. 3. 4. 5. 6. 7. 8.

Ex. The F major scale

The B flat (B♭) in the key signature indicates
that this note is to be played B flat (B♭)

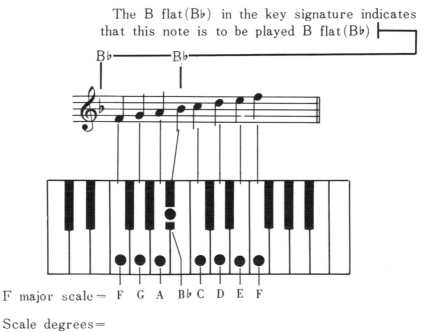

F major scale = F G A B♭ C D E F

Scale degrees=

Chords

A **chord** is defined as two or more notes played at the same time. In popular music a chord generally has a minimum of three notes.

The pitches which make up a chord are called **chord-tones**: any other pitches are called **non-chord-tones.**

Chords can be related to major scales by means of scale degrees.

The chord-tone upon which the rest of the chord is built is called the **root.**

The chord-tones of any chord can be related to the scale degrees of the major scale having the same keynote as the root of the chord.

Scale degrees=	1.	2.	3.	4.	5.	6.	7.	8.
	Keynote							Octave
Chord-tones=	R.	2.	3.	4.	5.	6.	7.	8.
	Root							

NOTE: **R** is used to differentiate clearly the root of the chord from the keynote of the scale when using numbers.

A **major triad** consists of the root, third and fifth scale degrees (R. 3. 5.).

Ex. C major triad

C major scale=	C	D	E	F	G	A	B	C
Scale degrees=	1.	2.	3.	4.	5.	6.	7.	8.
Chord-tones=	R.		3.		5.			

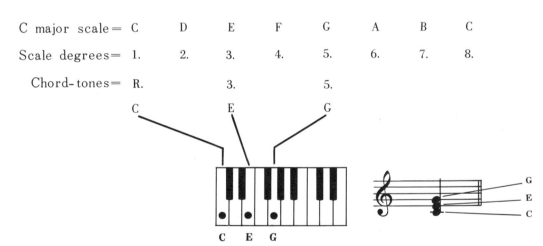

A **minor triad** consists of the root, flatted third and fifth scale degrees (R. b3. 5.).

Ex. C minor triad

C major scale=	C.	D.	E.	F.	G.	A.	B.	C.
Scale degrees=	1.	2.	3.	4.	5.	6.	7.	8.
Chord-tones=	R.		b3.		5.			

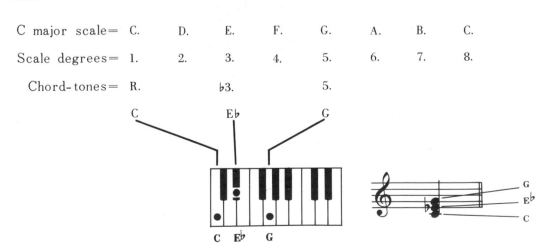

Inversions

A rearrangement of chord-tones is called an **inversion.**

A chord with the root as the lowest note is said to be in **root position;**

a chord with the third as the lowest note is said to be in the **first inversion;**

a chord with the fifth as the lowest note is said to be in the **second inversion,** etc.

However, the term **position** is often used instead of inversion: the relationship between **position** and **inversion** can be confusing and is shown below:

Ex. C major triad.

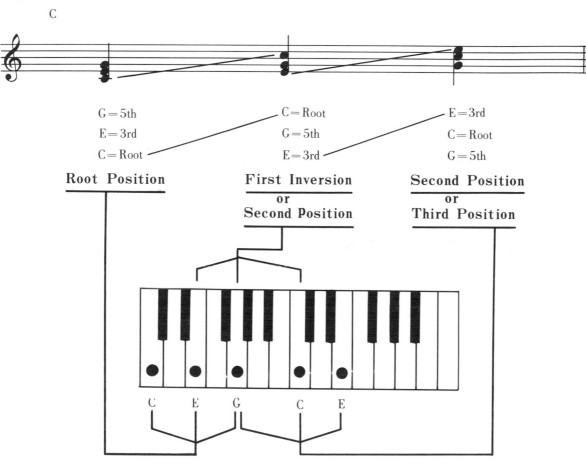

Since chord-tones can be rearranged into as many positions as there are chord-tones four-note chords will have four positions, five-note chords will have five positions, etc.

Specific chord positions can be indicated by using a slash mark (/) after the chord symbol and a letter, "R" for root position, or a number for other positions:

C/R = C major triad, root position; C/2 = C major triad, second position; C/3 = C major triad, third position, etc.

When the composer wishes to specify a particular bass note he may use a slash mark and a letter indicating the desired bass note:

C/E = C major triad (any position), E bass note; C/G = C major triad, G bass note, etc.

A specific chord position **and** a specific bass note can be indicated by using **two** slash marks, the letter or number after the first slash mark indicating the chord position, the letter after the second mark indicating the bass note:

C/2/G = C major triad, second position, G bass note, etc.

Since it is difficult for the average-sized hand to play more than four notes at a time only the top four notes of ninth (5-note) chords, eleventh (6-note) and thirteenth (7-note) chords will be inverted:

Ninth Chords

C9

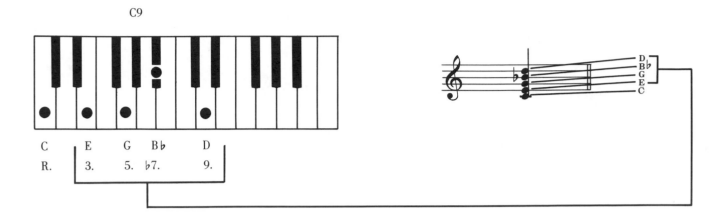

Eleventh chords

C11

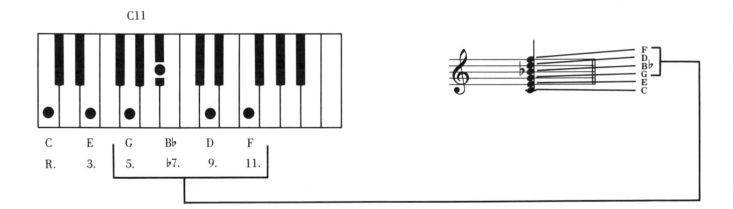

Thirteenth Chords

C13

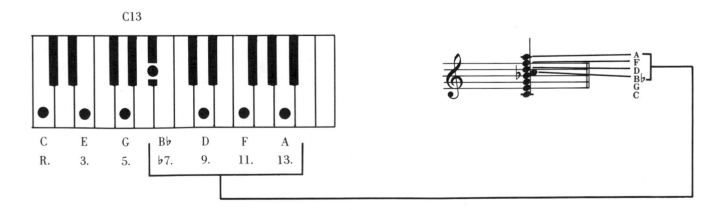

NOTE: ninth, eleventh and thirteenth chords are substitutes for common or dominant seventh chords; to simplify his playing the student may use the common or dominant seventh chord instead of the ninth, eleventh or thirteenth.

On the following pages chords and their construction by means of scale degrees are shown.

Although the examples given are for C chords any root can be used.

The most common chord symbols will also be given.

For the examples in C the C major scale should be kept in mind:

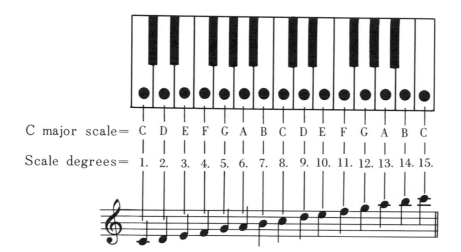

Major Triad

Chord-tones = R., 3., 5.

Chord symbol = C (capital letter only)

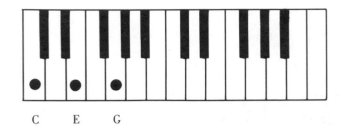

Minor Triad

Chord-tones = R., ♭3., 5.

Chord symbols = Cm or C—

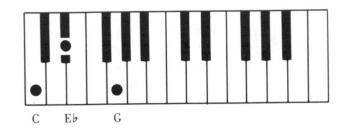

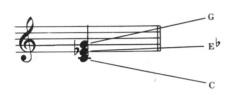

Augmented Triad

Chord-tones = R., 3., ♯5

Chord symbols = C+5, C+, C(♯5)

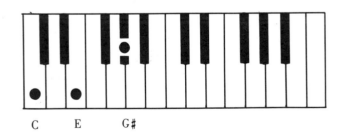

Lowered Fifth Triad

Chord-tones = R., 3., ♭5.

Chord symbols = C—5, C(♭5)

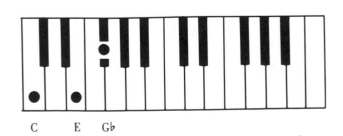

Diminished Triad

Chord-tones = R., ♭3., ♭5.

Chord symbols = Cdim., C°

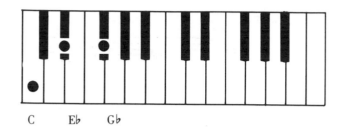

C   E♭   G♭

G♭
E♭
C

Major Seventh Chord

Chord-tones = R., 3., 5., 7.

Chord symbols = Cmaj.7, CM7. C

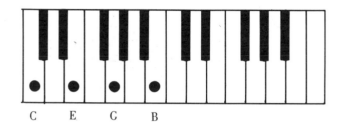

C   E   G   B

B
G
E
C

Dominant Seventh Chord

Chord-tones = R., 3., 5., ♭7.

Chord symbol = C7

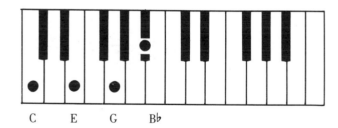

C   E   G   B♭

B♭
G
E
C

Minor Seventh Chord

Chord-tones = R., ♭3., 5., ♭7.

Chord symbol = Cm7

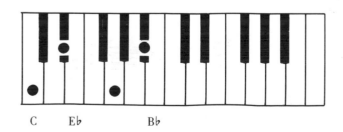

C   E♭   B♭

B♭
G
E♭
C

Major Sixth Chord

Chord-tones = R.,   3.,   5.,   6.

Chord symbol—C6

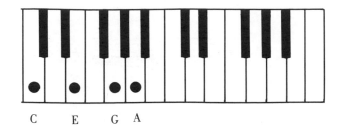

Minor Sixth Chord

Chord-tones = R., ♭3.,   5.,   6.

Chord symbol = Cm6

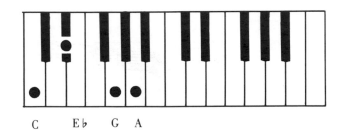

Diminished Seventh Chord

Chord-tones = R.,   ♭3., ♭5.,   ♭♭7.

Chord symbol = Cdim. 7

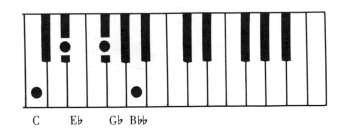

Minor Seventh Lowered Fifth Chord, or Half-Diminished Chord

Chord-tones = R.,   ♭3., ♭5.,   ♭7.

Chord symbols = Cm7-5, Cø

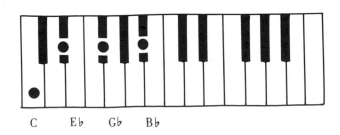

Seventh Augmented Fifth Chord, or Augmented Seventh Chord

Chord-tones = R., 3., ♯5., ♭7

Chord symbols = C7+5, C7aug. 5

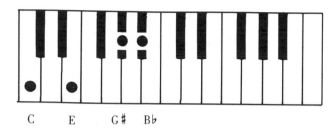

Seventh Lowered Fifth Chord

Chord-tones = R., 3., ♭5., ♭7

Chord symbols = C7-5, C7♭5, C7(♭5)

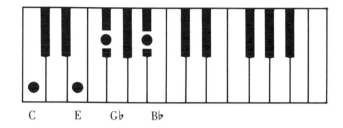

Seventh Suspended Fourth Chord

Chord-tones — R., 4., 5., ♭7

Chord symbol = C7sus. 4

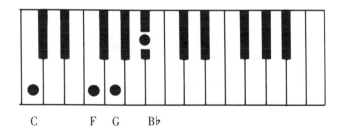

Major Seventh Flatted Third, Flatted Fifth Chord

Chord-tones = R., ♭3., ♭5., 7.

Chord symbols = CM7 ♭3 ♭5, Cmaj.7, ♭3, ♭5

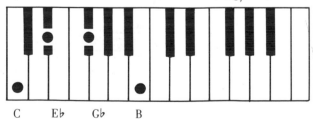

Major Seventh Flatted Third, Augmented Fifth Chord

Chord-tones = R., ♭3., #5., 7.

Chord symbols = CM7 ♭3 #5, Cmaj. 7, ♭3, #5

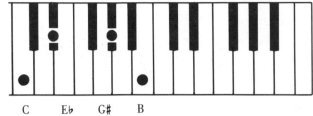

C   E♭   G#   B

Major Ninth Chord

Chord-tones = R., 3., 5., 7., 9

Chord symbol = Cmaj. 9

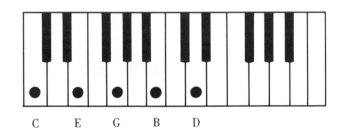

C   E   G   B   D

Ninth Chord

Chord-tones = R., 3., 5., ♭7., 9.

Chord symbol = C9

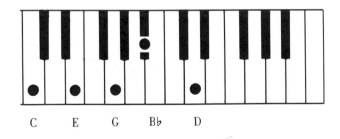

C   E   G   B♭   D

Ninth Augmented Fifth Chord

Chord-tones = R., 3., #5., ♭7., 9.

Chord symbols = C9, #5, C9, +5.

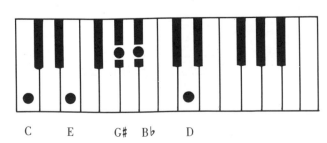

C   E   G#   B♭   D

Ninth Lowered Fifth Chord

Chord-tones = R., 3., ♭5., ♭7., 9.

Chord symbols = C9−5, C9, ♭5.

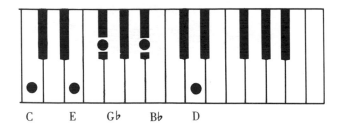

C   E   G♭   B♭   D

Minor Ninth Chord

Chord-tones = R., ♭3., 5., ♭7., 9.

Chord symbol = Cm9

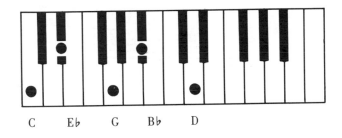

C   E♭   G   B♭   D

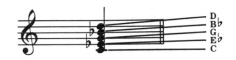

Minor Ninth Augmented Fifth Chord

Chord-tones = R., ♭3., ♯5., ♭7., 9.

Chord symbols = Cm9+5, Cm9 ♯5

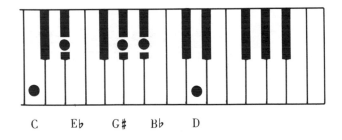

C   E♭   G♯   B♭   D

Minor Ninth Lowered Fifth Chord

Chord-tones = R., ♭3., ♭5., ♭7., 9.

Chord symbols = Cm9−5, Cm9, ♭5.

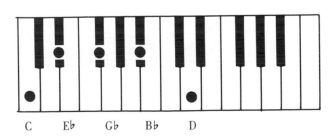

C   E♭   G♭   B♭   D

Seventh Flatted Ninth Chord

Chord-tones = R., 3., 5., ♭7., ♭9.

Chord symbols = C7,♭9, C7-9

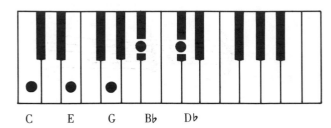

Eleventh Chord

Chord-tones = R., 3., 5., ♭7., 9., 11.

Chord symbol = C11

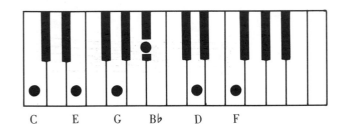

Eleventh Flatted Ninth Chord

Chord-tones = R., 3., 5., ♭7., ♭9., 11.

Chord symbols = C11,♭9, C11-9

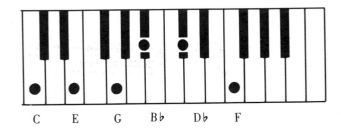
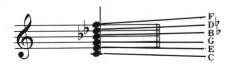

Eleventh Augmented Fifth Chord

Chord-tones = R., 3., ♯5., ♭7., 9., 11.

Chord symbols = C11, ♯5, C11, +5.

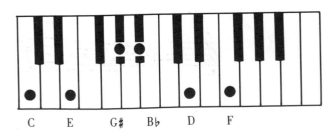
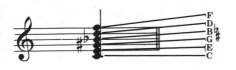

Thirteenth Chord

Chord-tones = R., 3., 5., ♭7., 9., 11., 13.

Chord symbol = C13.

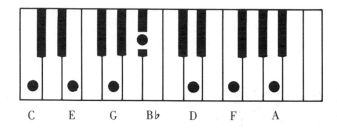 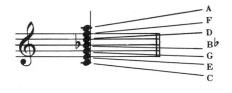

Thirteenth Flatted Ninth Chord

Chord-tones = R., 3., 5., ♭7., ♭9., 11., 13.

Chord symbols = C13, ♭9, C13-9

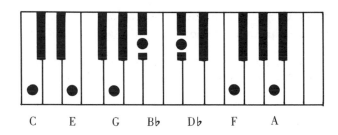 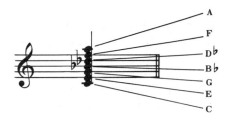

Seven Six Chord

Chord-tones = R., 3., 5., 6., ♭7.

Chord symbols = C7, 6, C7/6.

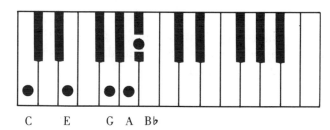 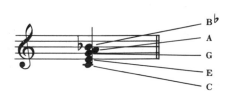

Six Nine Chord

Chord-tones = R., 3., 5., 6., 9.

Chord symbol = C6, 9.

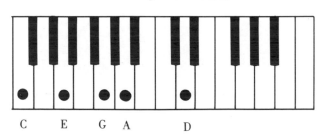 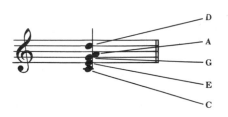

Enharmonic Notation

The musical alphabet is used to label the white keys only. The black keys derive their names from the adjacent white keys.

The following chart shows how the keys are named:

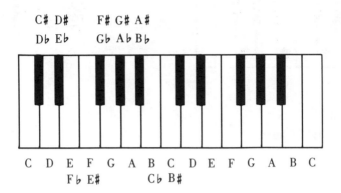

Notice that a black key can have two names, such as C#-Db. The fact that a key can have more than one name is called **enharmonic notation,** meaning equivalent names for the same pitch.

Notice that certain white keys can have two names, such as E-Fb. Enharmonic notation is used to preserve certain musical relationships, such as the whole-step and half-step relationships between the scale degrees of a major scale.

Ex. F# Major Scale.

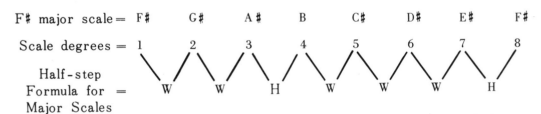

Because there must be a half-step between the 7th and 8th scale degrees the white key which is a half-step down from F# is now called E# instead of F natural.

Enharmonic notation is quite often used in writing music in order to make it easier to read in certain situations.

In a diminished seventh chord the diminished seventh itself is theoretically written as the double-flatted seventh scale degree (♭♭7): however, the double-flatted seventh is often difficult to read and the enharmonic equivalent, the major sixth scale degree, is often used instead:

Ex. C Diminished Seventh Chord

Chord-tones = R., ♭3., ♭5., ♭♭7.

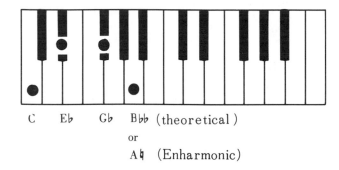

C   E♭   G♭   B♭♭ (theoretical)
or
A♮ (Enharmonic)

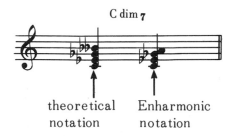

theoretical notation   Enharmonic notation

In this book the correct theoretical notation will be used throughout.

NOTE: in the above example, if the diminished seventh chord were built on C♭ instead of C, the chord-tones would have been C♭, E♭♭, G♭♭, B♭♭♭ (B triple flat !!): conceivably, E♭♭, G♭♭ B♭♭♭ could be written with their enharmonic equivalents, D , F , and A :

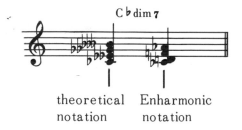

theoretical notation   Enharmonic notation

The fingers can be numbered with the thumb of each hand counted as one, the little finger as five:

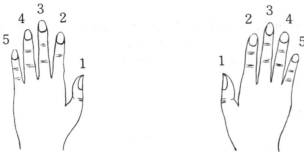

The scales on the following pages should be practised with strict adherence to the fingerings given, the thumb passing under the other fingers in ascending while the other fingers pass over the thumb descending:

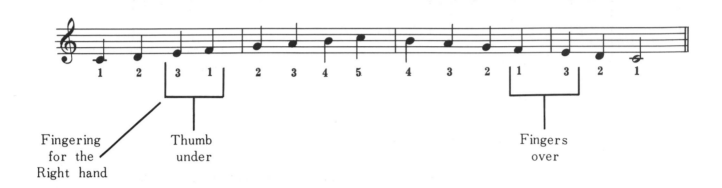

8va means play an octave higher than written.
Loco means return to the original octave.

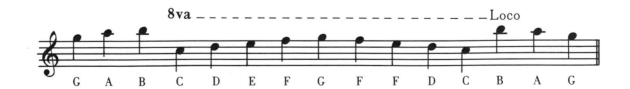

When the notes written in the bass clef climb too high on the staff the treble clef can be used to eliminate the need for leger lines:

In the following pages major scales are presented by means of keyboard diagrams and annotation on the Grand Staff.

Ex. C Major Scale.

Key of C Major

C Major Scale in One Octave:

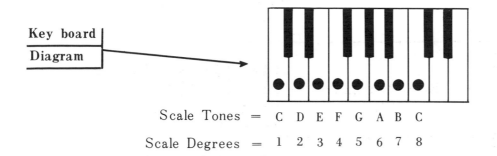

Scale Tones = C D E F G A B C

Scale Degrees = 1 2 3 4 5 6 7 8

Annotation:

Fingering for the Right Hand

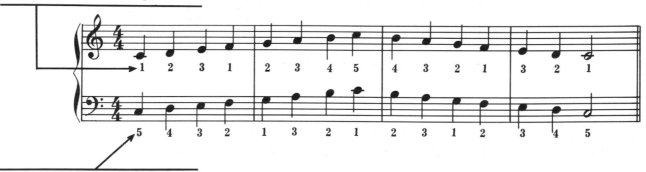

Fingering for the Left Hand

In the following pages the chords most commonly found in popular music are presented by means of keyboard diagrams.

Ex. C Major Triad.

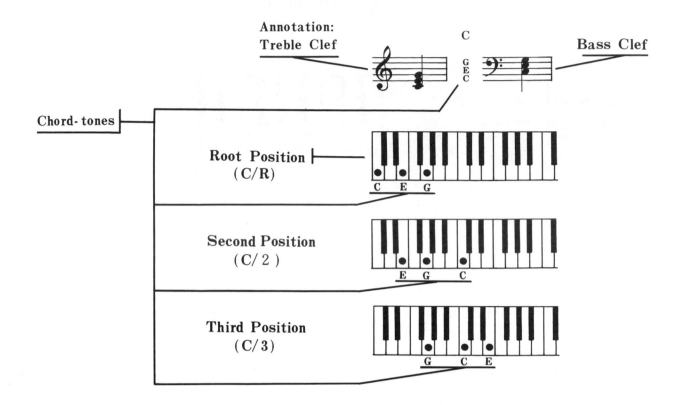

NOTE: another keyboard diagram for the fourth position of four-note chords and inversions of the top four notes of five-, six-, and seven-note chords will be given where needed.

To conserve space fingerings for the chords are not shown.

A simple rule for fingering the chords is "use whatever fingering is comfortable and convenient."

Key of C Major

C Major Scale in One Octave

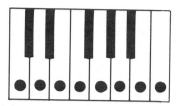

Scale Tones = C D E F G A B C
Scale Degrees = 1 2 3 4 5 6 7 8

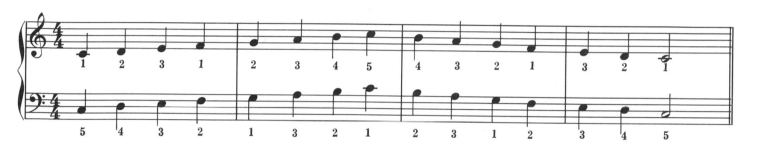

C Major Scale in Two Octaves

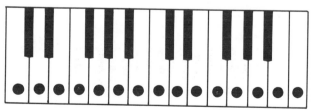

Scale Tones = C D E F G A B C D E F G A B C
Scale degrees = 1 2 3 4 5 6 7 8 9 10 11 12 13 14 15

26

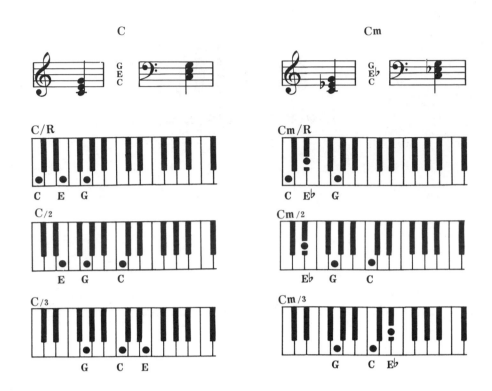

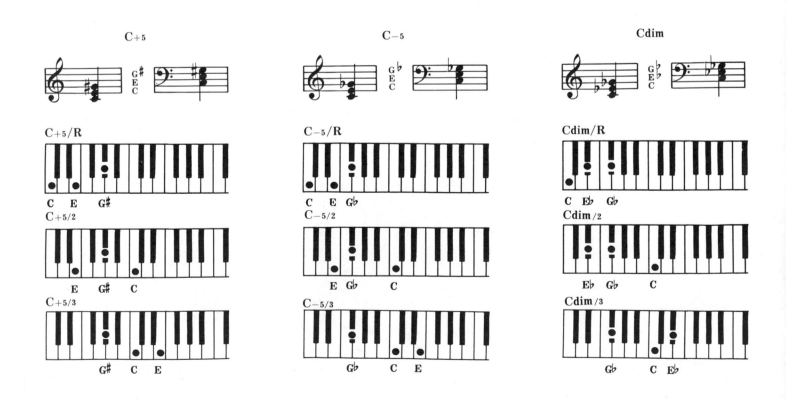

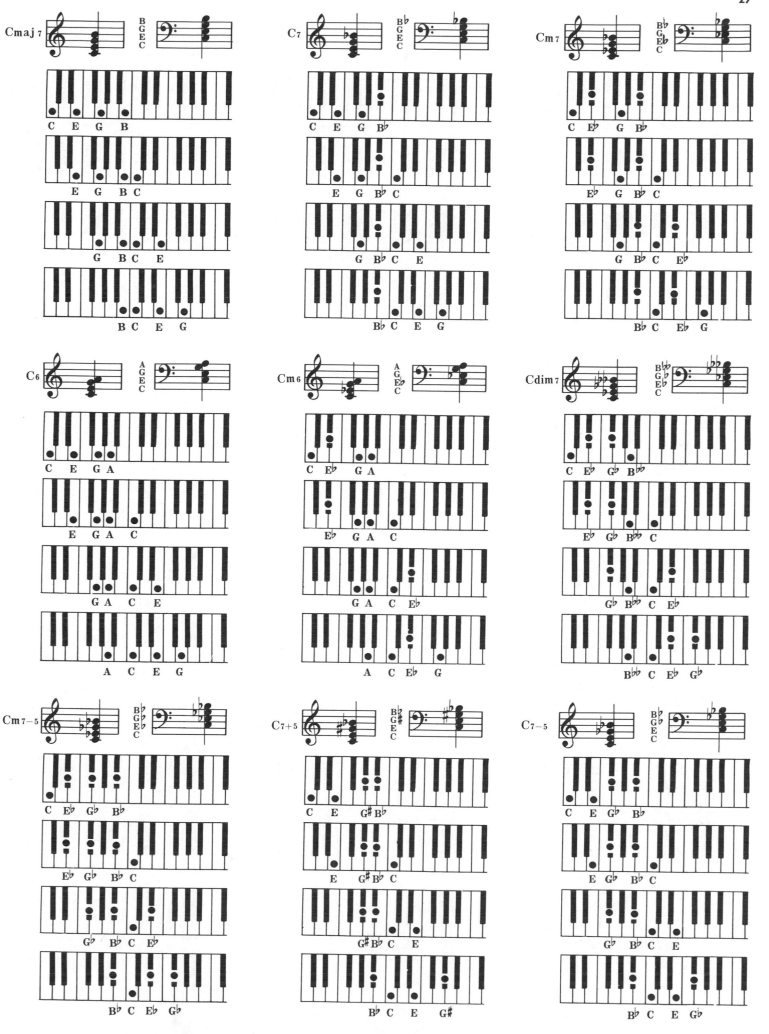

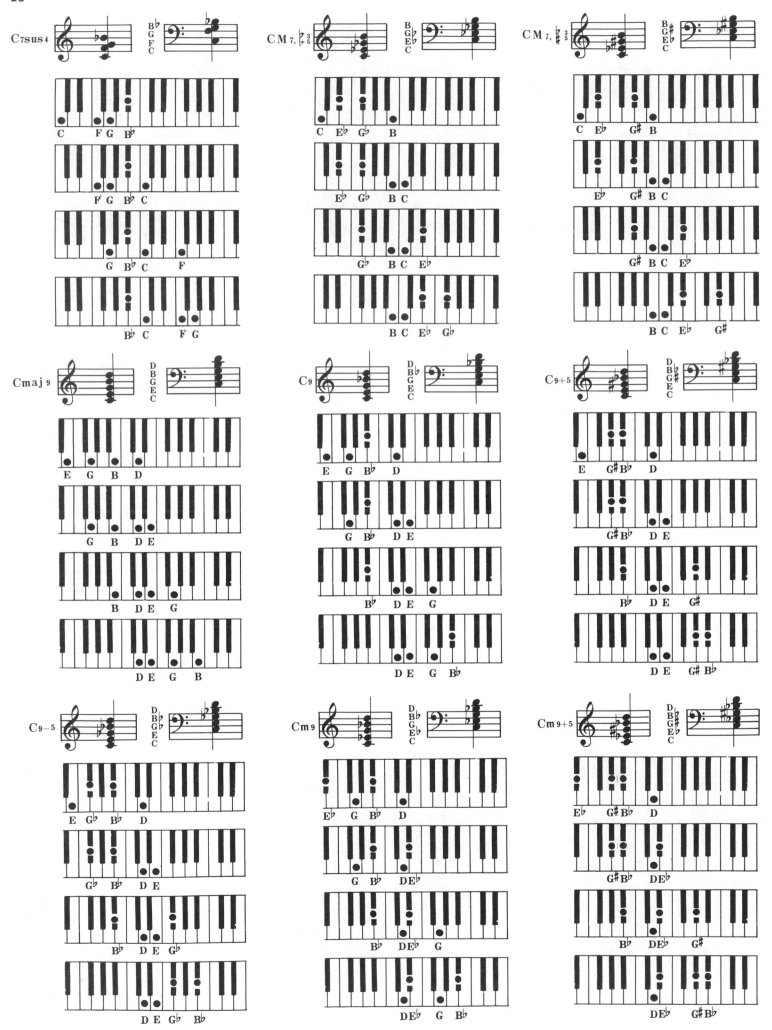

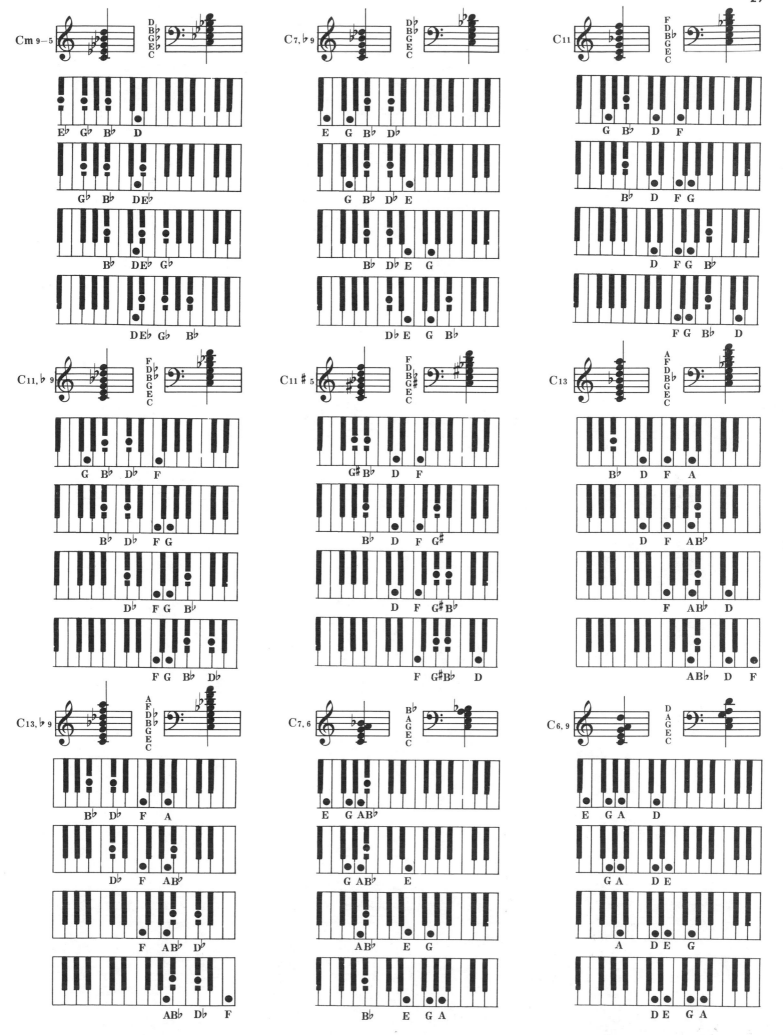

Key of D♭ Major (identical to C♯)

D♭ Major Scale in One Octave

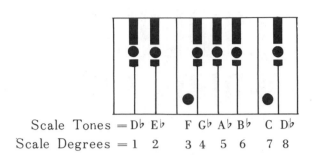

Scale Tones = D♭ E♭   F G♭ A♭ B♭   C D♭
Scale Degrees = 1   2   3 4 5 6   7 8

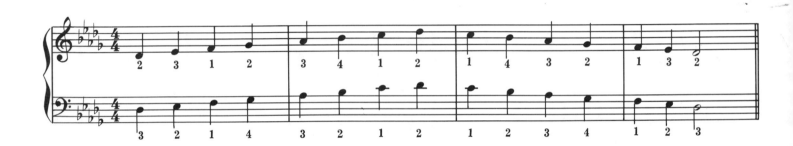

D♭ Major Scale in Two Octaves

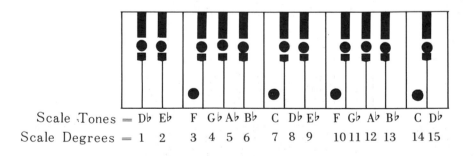

Scale Tones = D♭ E♭   F G♭ A♭ B♭   C D♭ E♭   F G♭ A♭ B♭   C D♭
Scale Degrees = 1   2   3 4 5 6   7 8 9   10 11 12 13   14 15

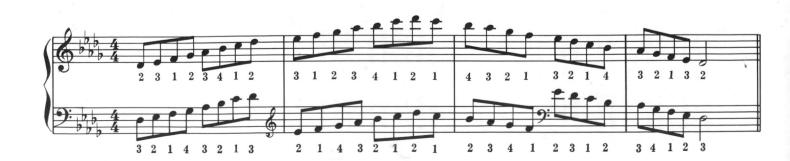

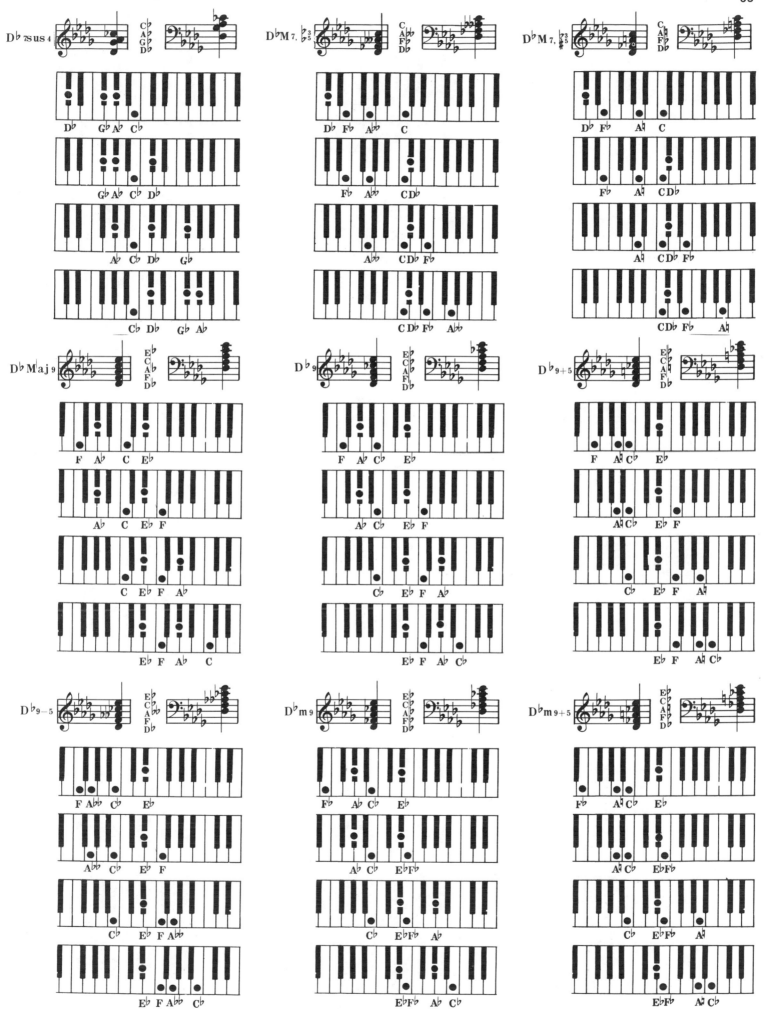

D♭ m 9–5

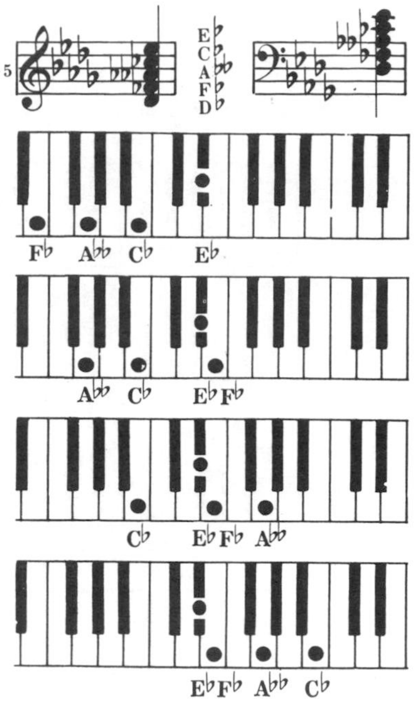

D♭ 7, ♭9

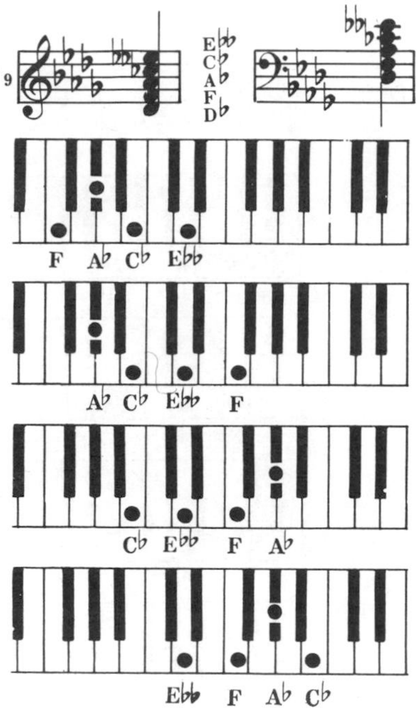

D♭ 11

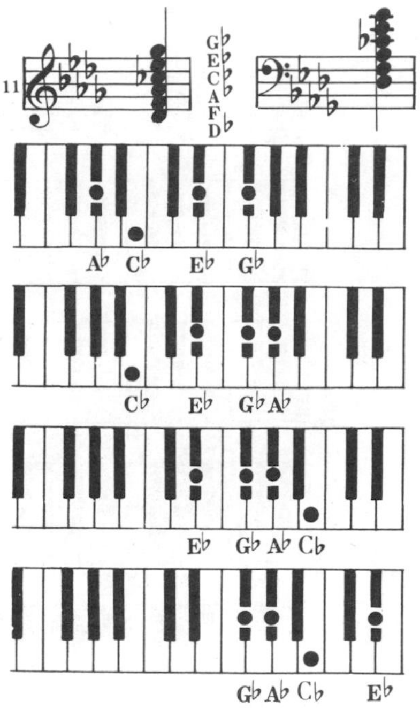

D♭ 11, ♭9

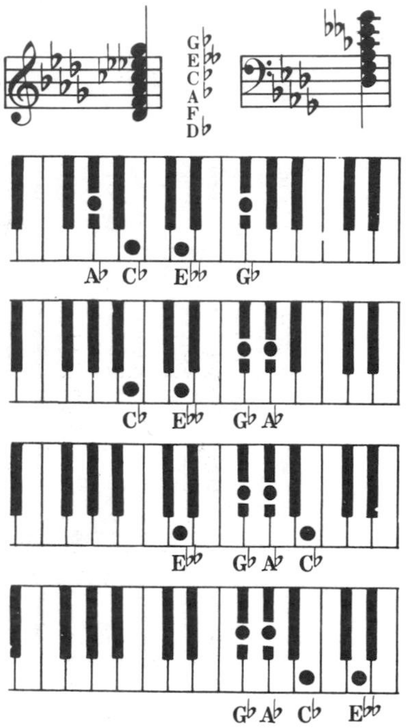

D♭ 11, ♯5

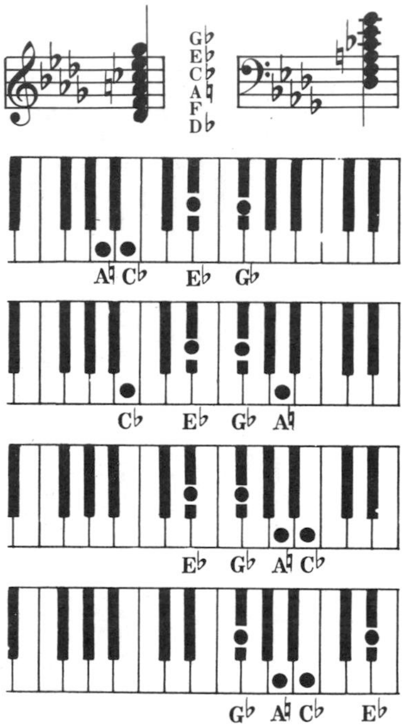

D♭ 13

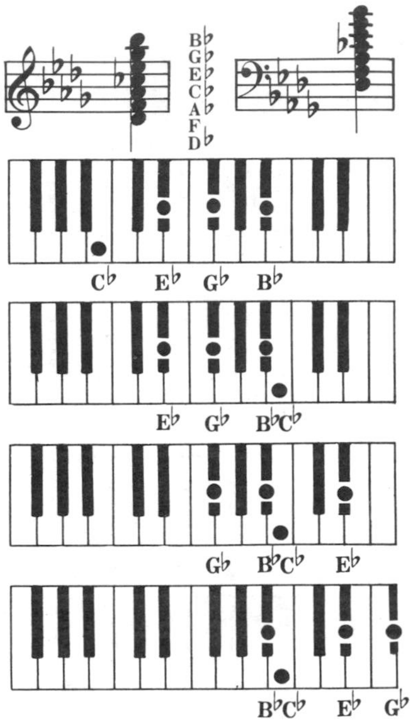

D♭ 13, ♭9

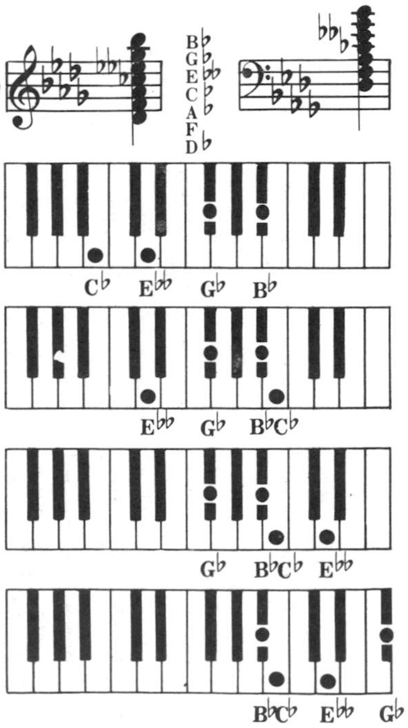

D♭ 7. 6

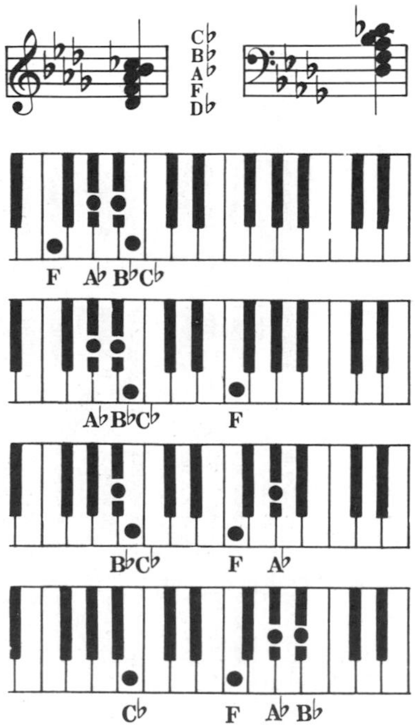

D♭ 6, 9

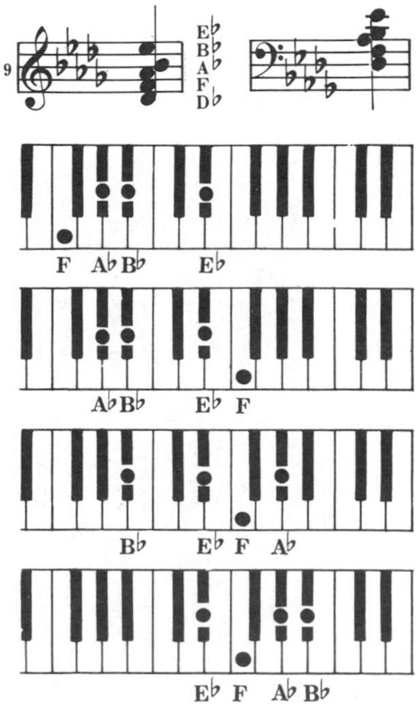

Key of D Major

D Major Scale in One Octave

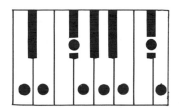

Scale Tones = D E F♯ G A B C♯ D

Scale Degrees = 1 2 3 4 5 6 7 8

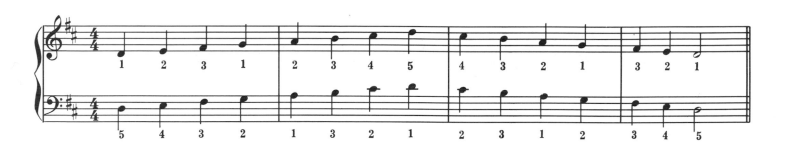

D Major Scale in Two Octaves

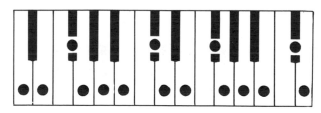

Scale Tones = D E F♯ G A B C♯ D E F♯ G A B C♯ D

Scale Degrees = 1 2 3 4 5 6 7 8 9 10 11 12 13 14 15

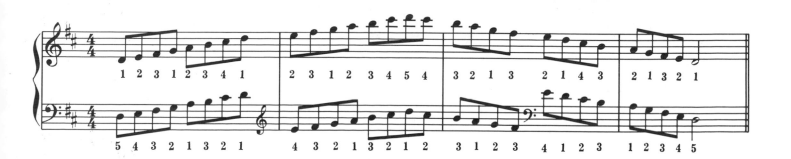

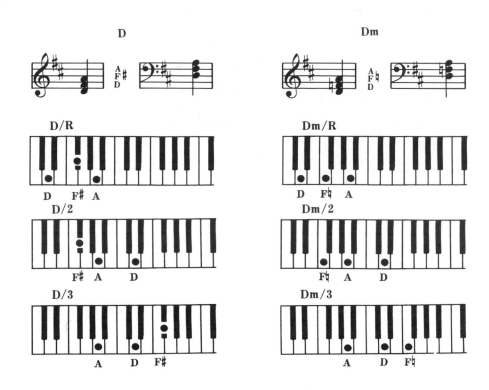

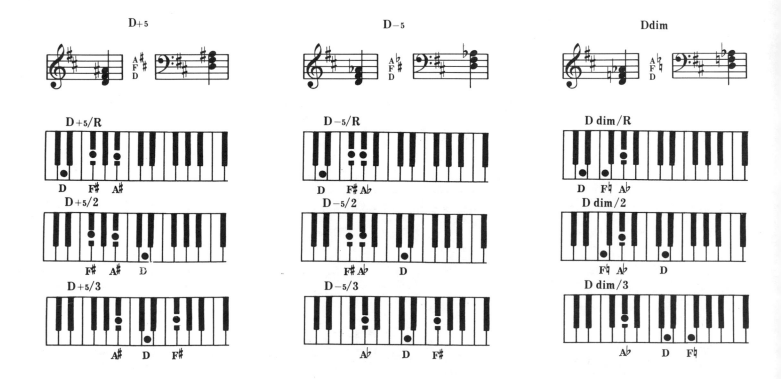

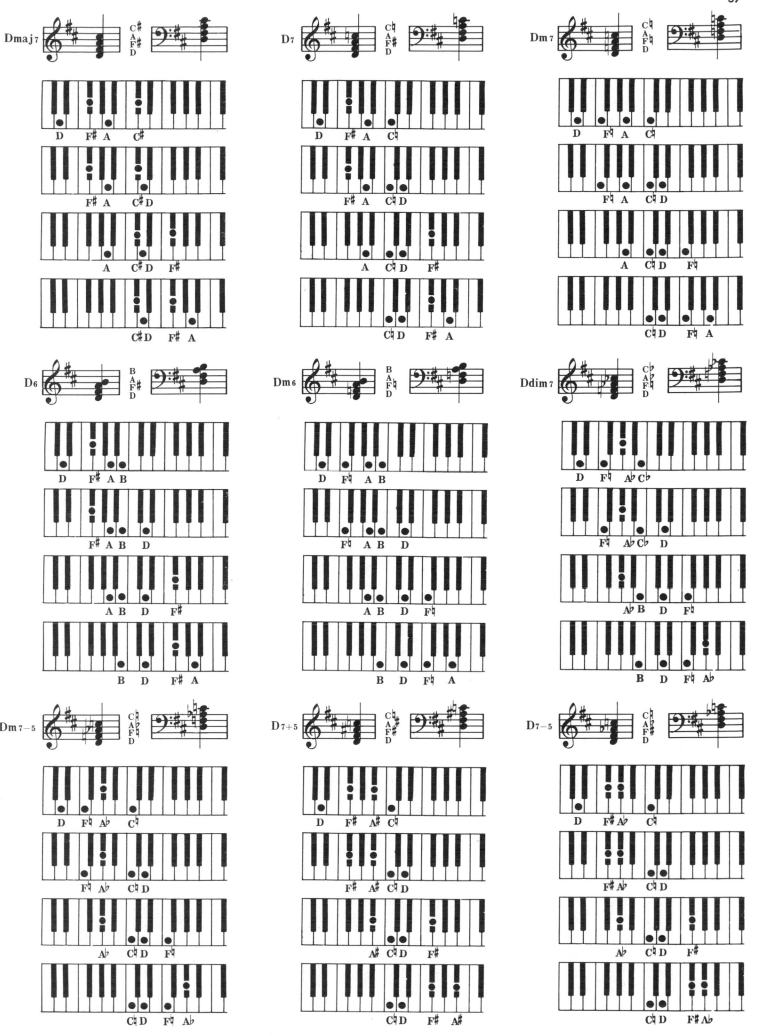

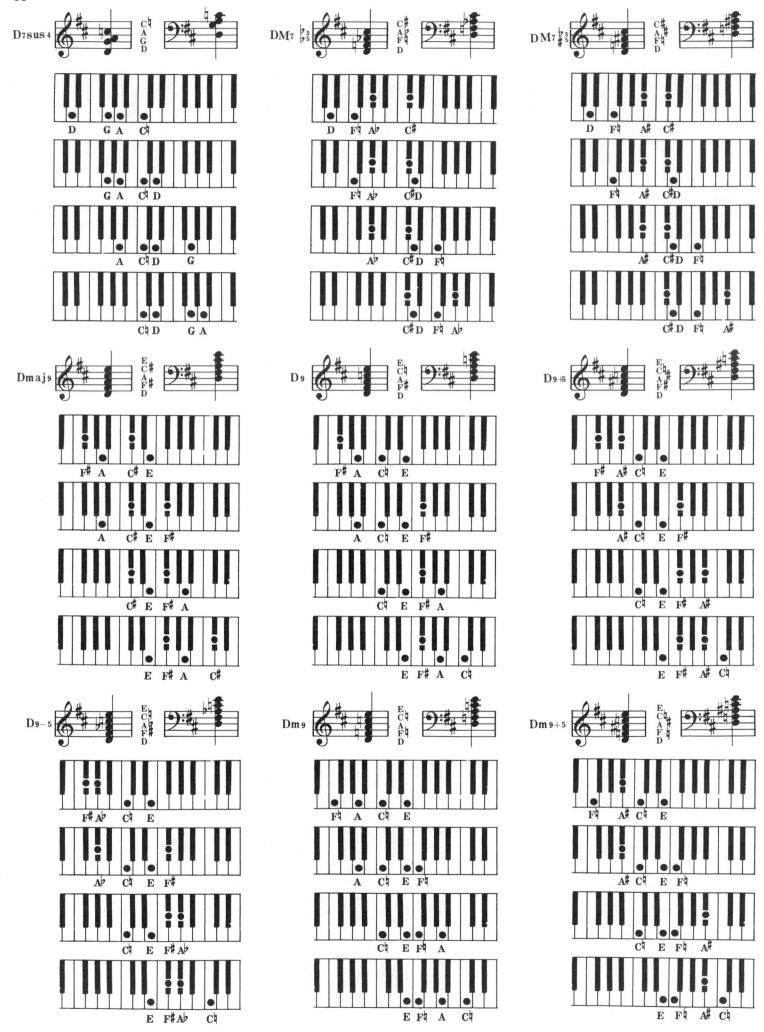

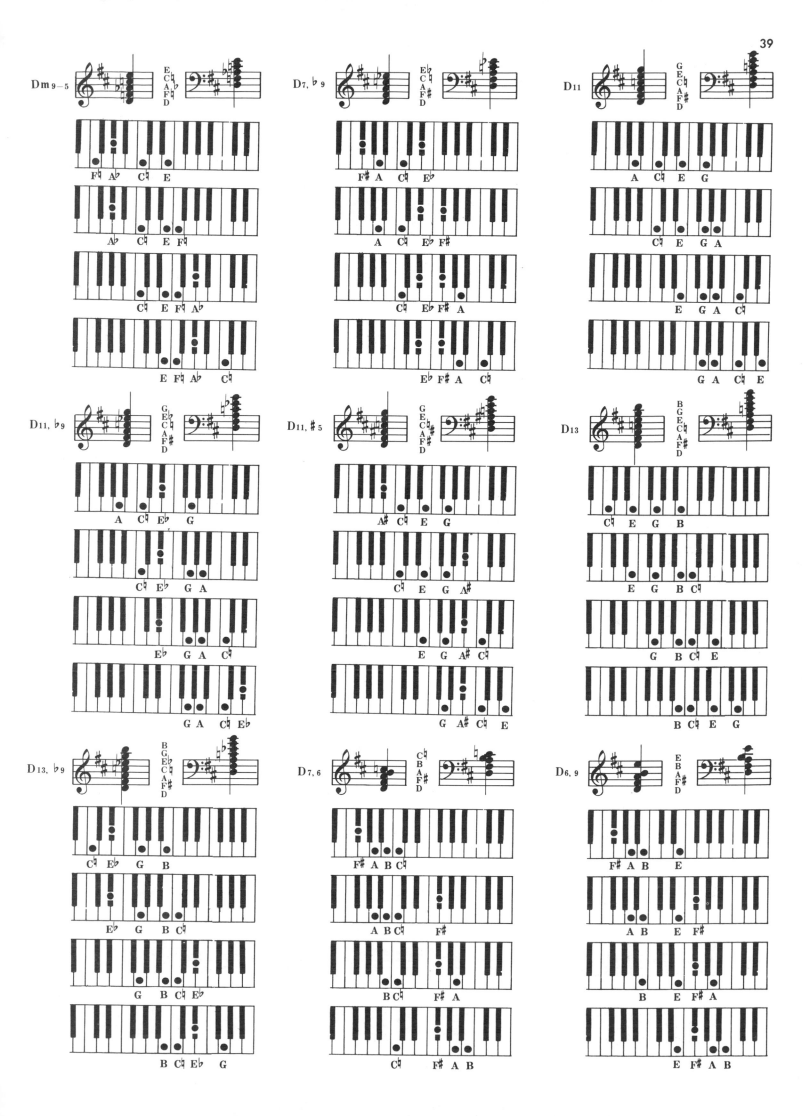

Key of E♭ Major

E♭ Major Scale in One Octave

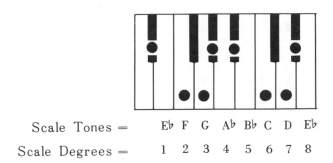

Scale Tones =	E♭	F	G	A♭	B♭	C	D	E♭
Scale Degrees =	1	2	3	4	5	6	7	8

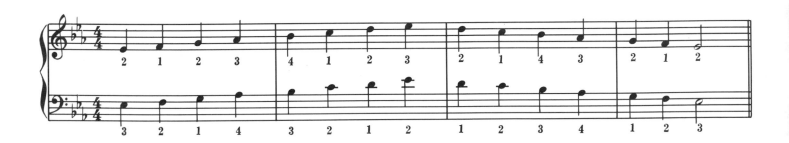

E♭ Major Scale in Two Octaves

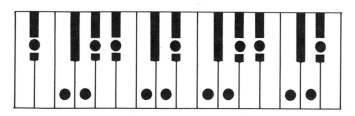

Scale Tones =	E♭	F	G	A♭	B♭	C	D	E♭	F	G	A♭	B♭	C	D	E♭
Scale Degrees =	1	2	3	4	5	6	7	8	9	10	11	12	13	14	15

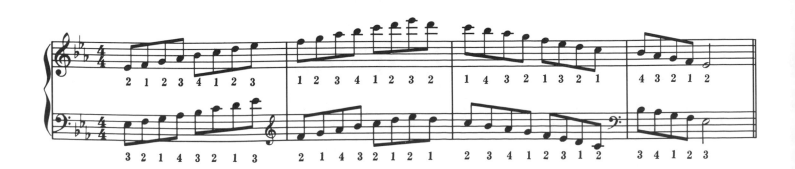

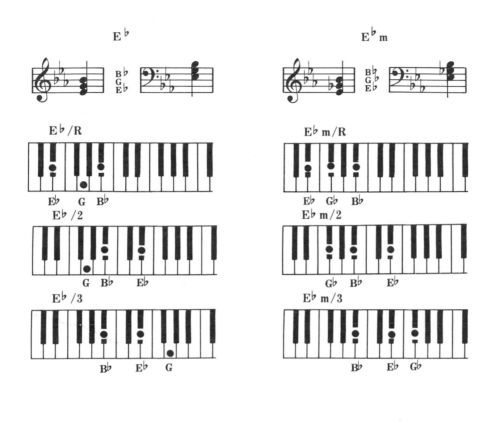

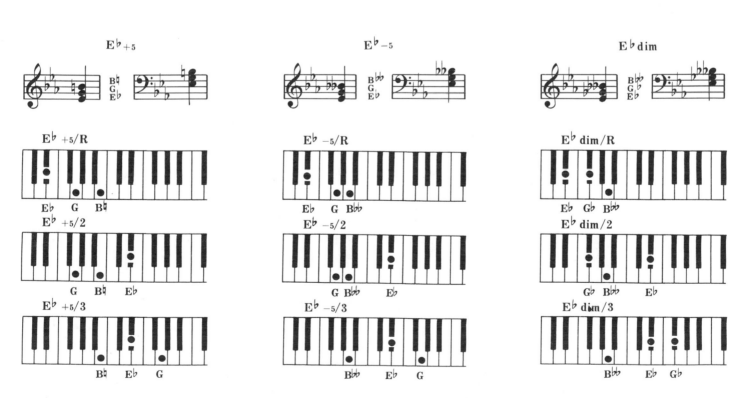

E♭maj7

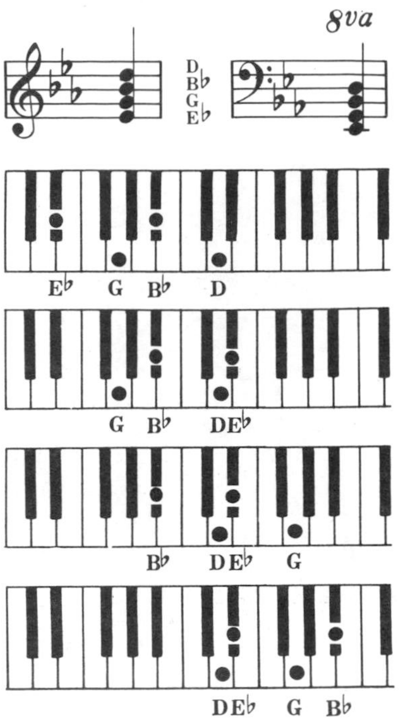

E♭7

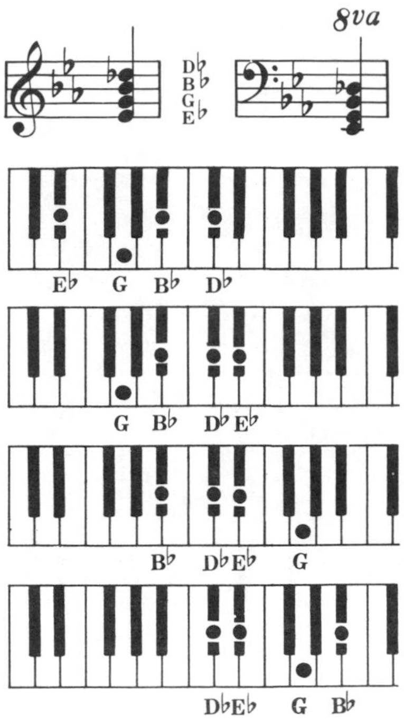

E♭m7

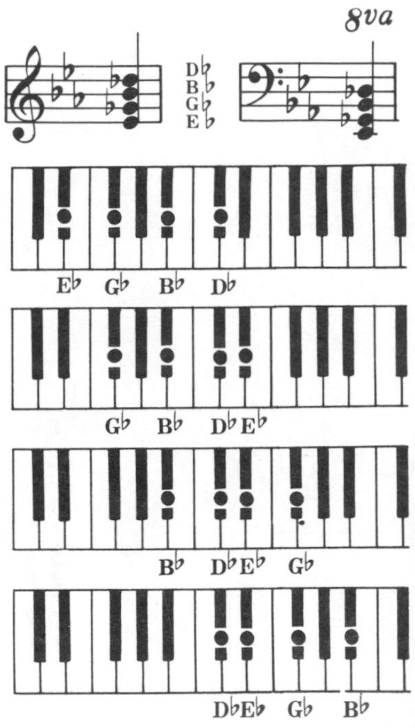

E♭6

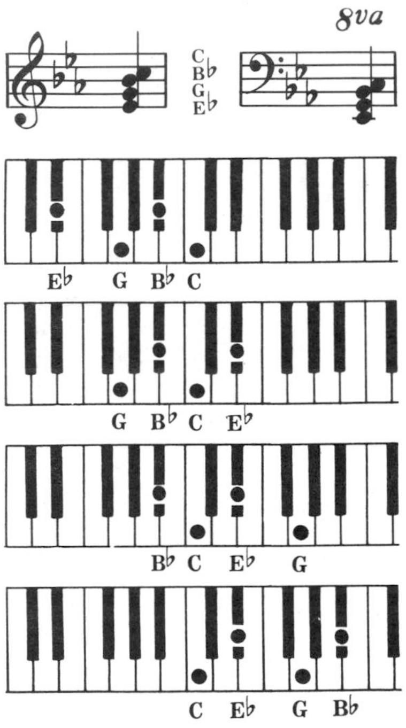

E♭m6

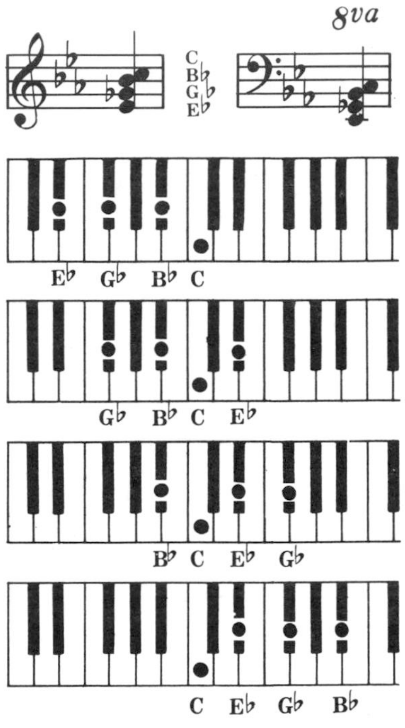

E♭dim7

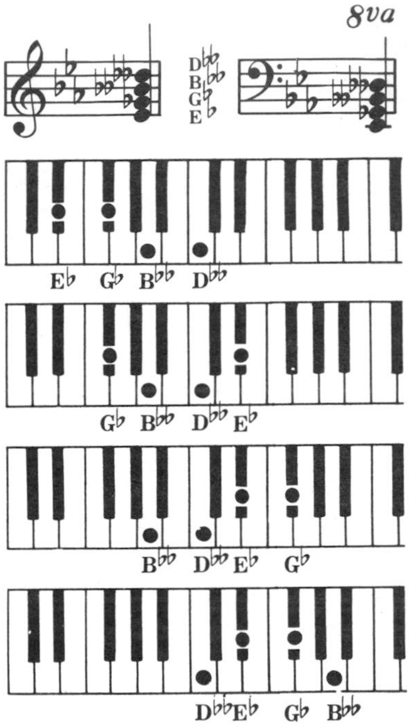

E♭m7−5

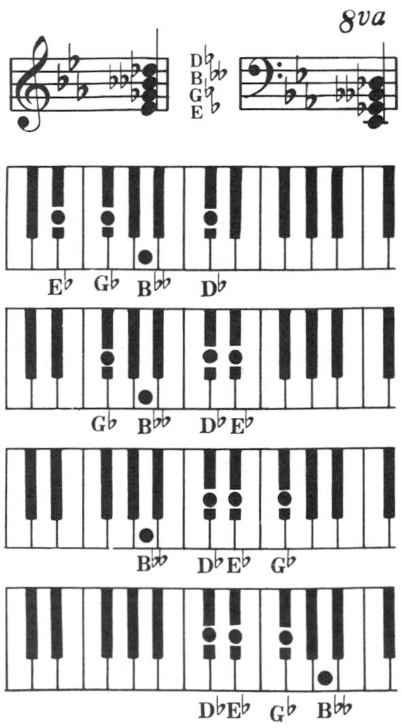

E♭7+5

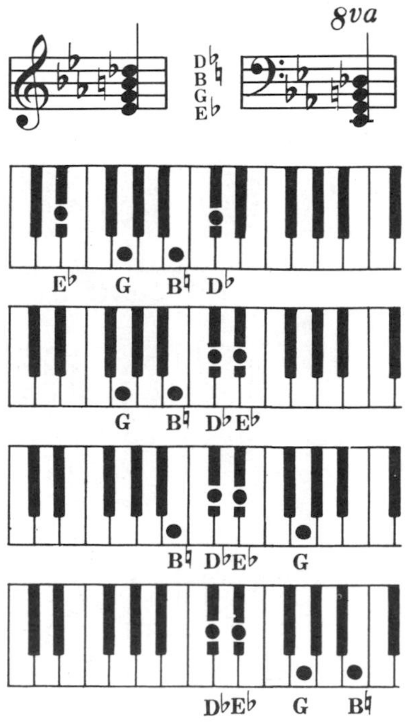

E♭7−5

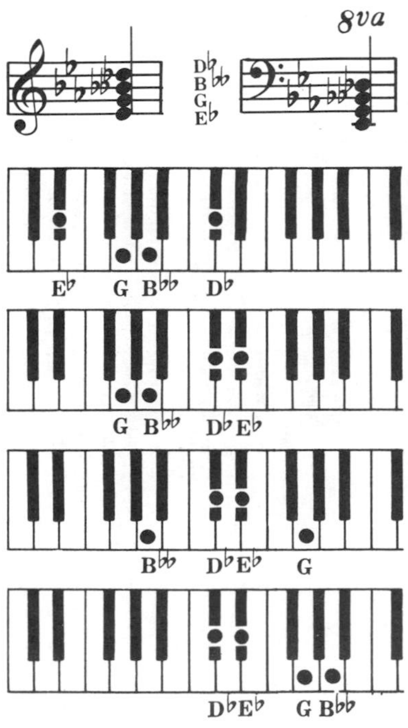

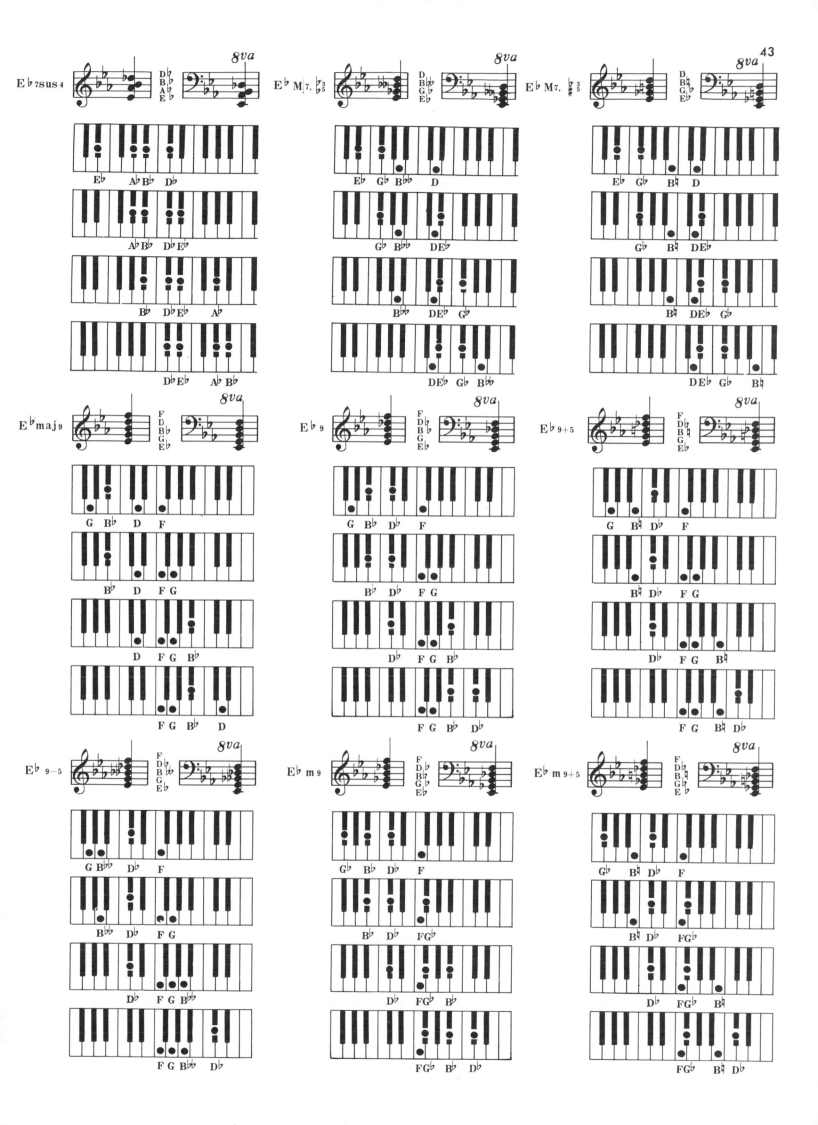

E♭ m9−5

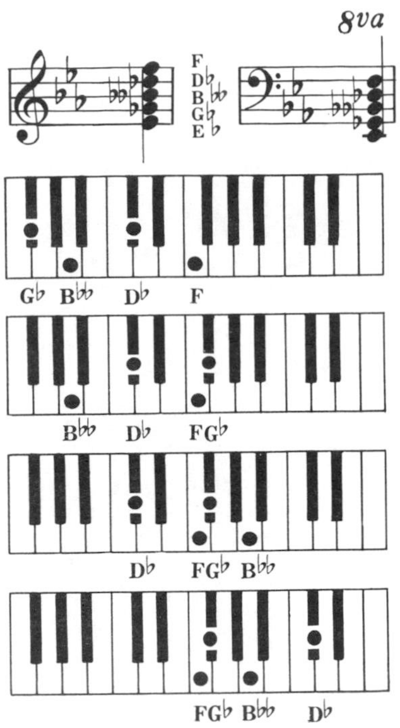

E♭ 7,♭9

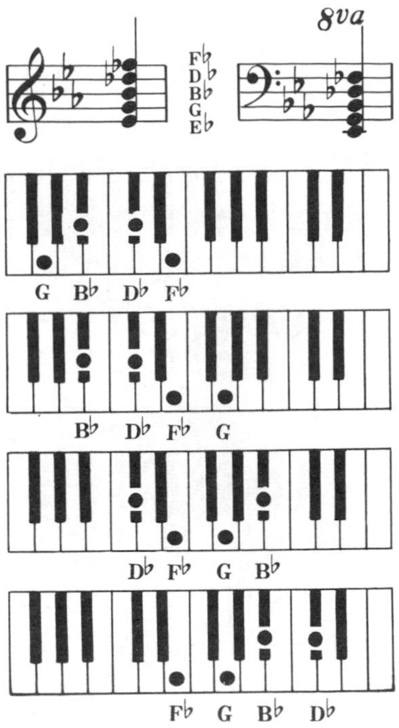

E♭ 11

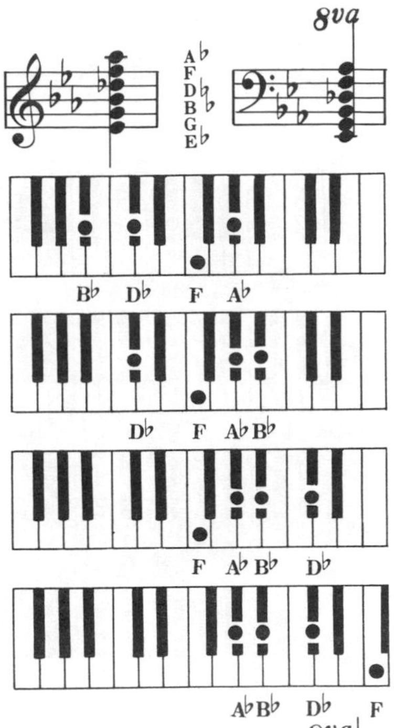

E♭ 11,♭9

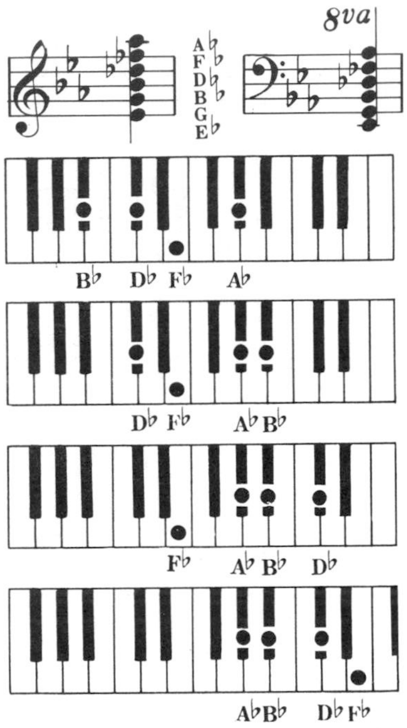

E♭ 11,♯5

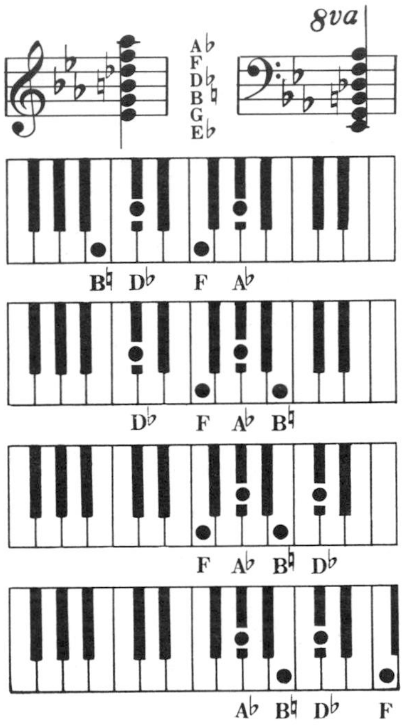

E♭ 13

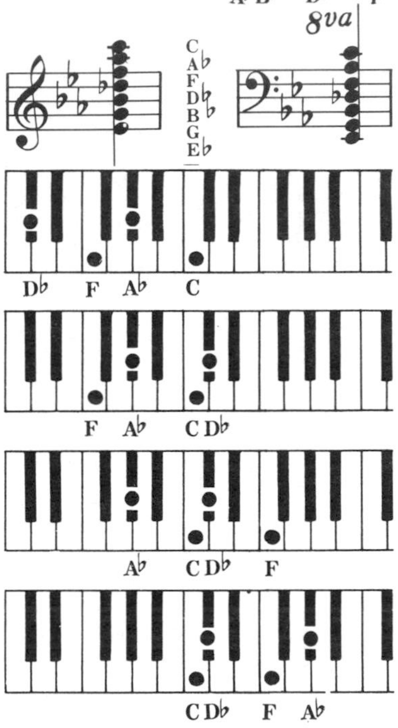

E♭ 13,♭9

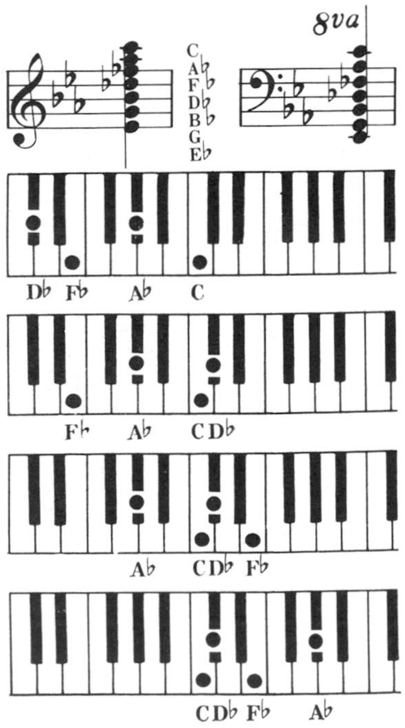

E♭ 7, 6

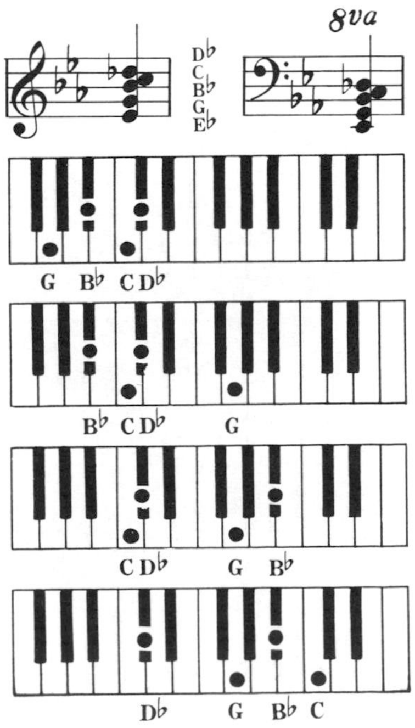

E♭ 6, 9

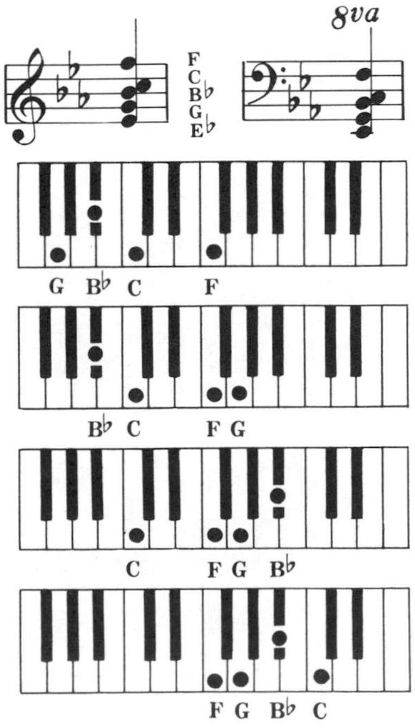

Key of E Major

E Major Scale in One Octave

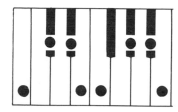

Scale Tones = E F♯ G♯ A B C♯ D♯ E

Scale Degrees = 1 2 3 4 5 6 7 8

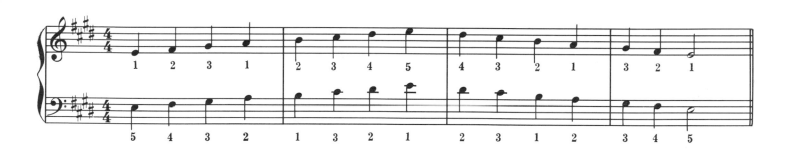

E Major Scale in Two Octaves

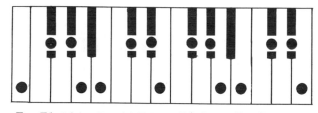

Scale Tones = E F♯ G♯ A B C♯ D♯ E F♯ G♯ A B C♯ D♯ E

Scale Degrees = 1 2 3 4 5 6 7 8 9 10 11 12 13 14 15

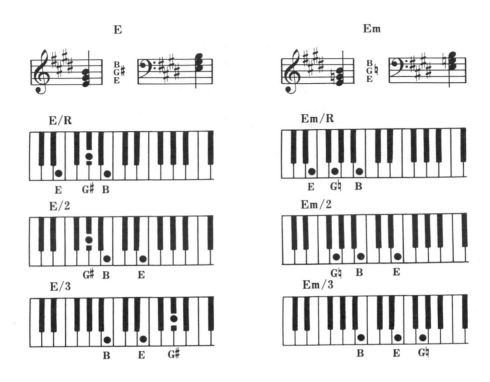

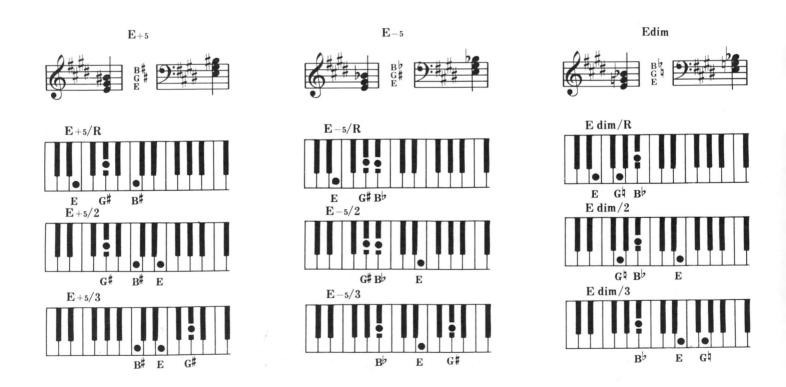

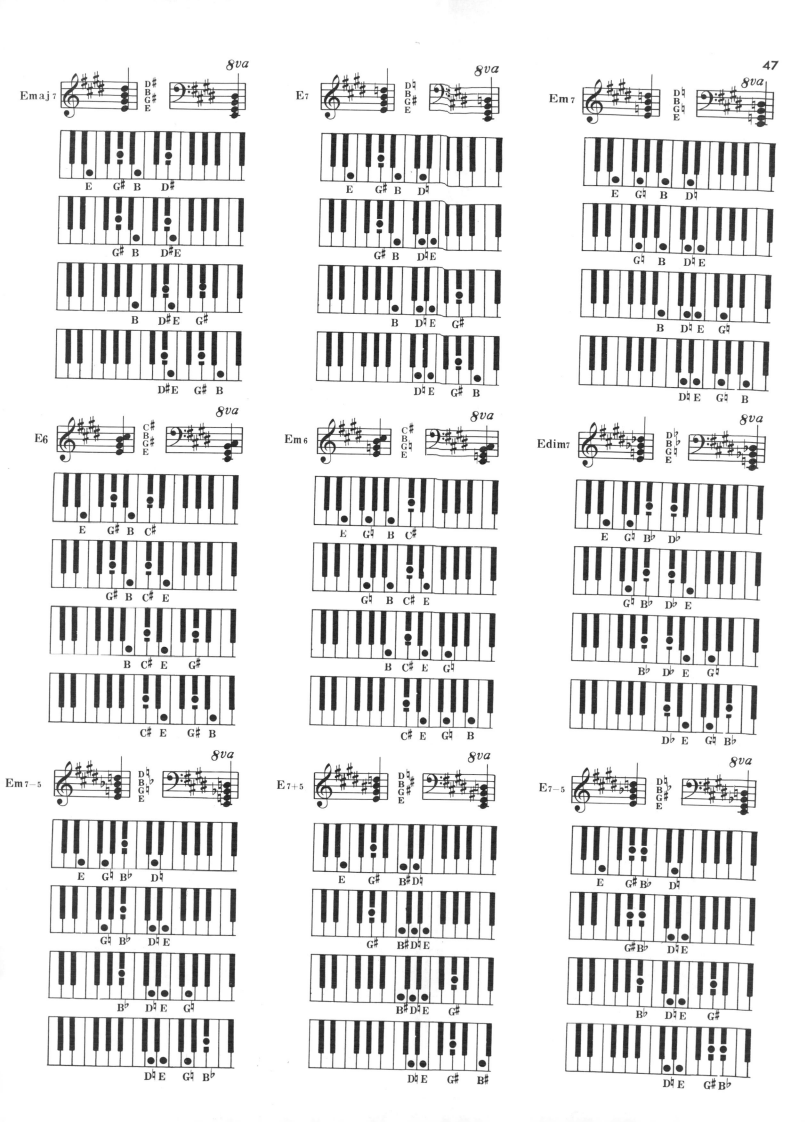

48

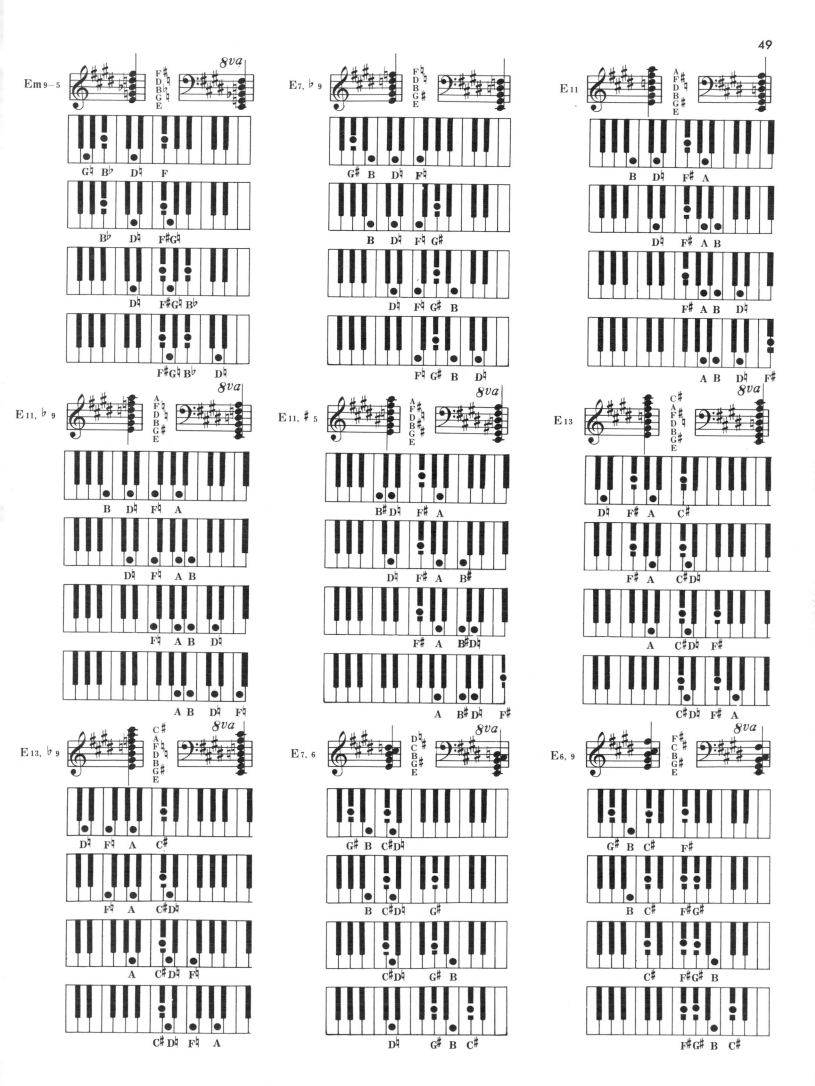

Key of F Major

F Major Scale in One Octave

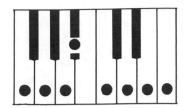

Scale Tones = F G A Bb C D E F
Scale Degrees = 1 2 3 4 5 6 7 8

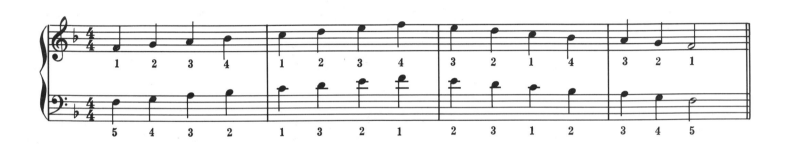

F Major Scale in Two Octaves

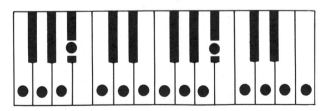

Scale Tones = F G A Bb C D E F G A Bb C D E F
Scale Degrees = 1 2 3 4 5 6 7 8 9 10 11 12 13 14 15

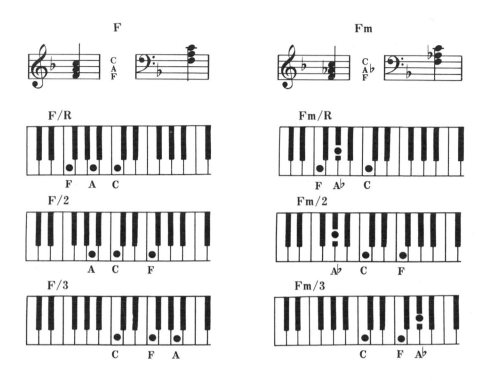

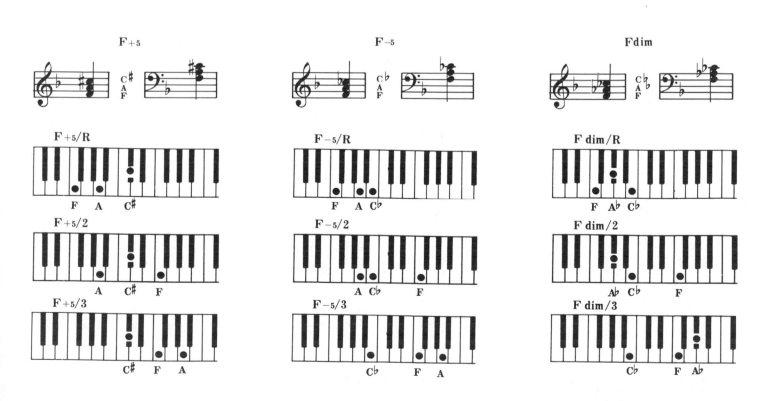

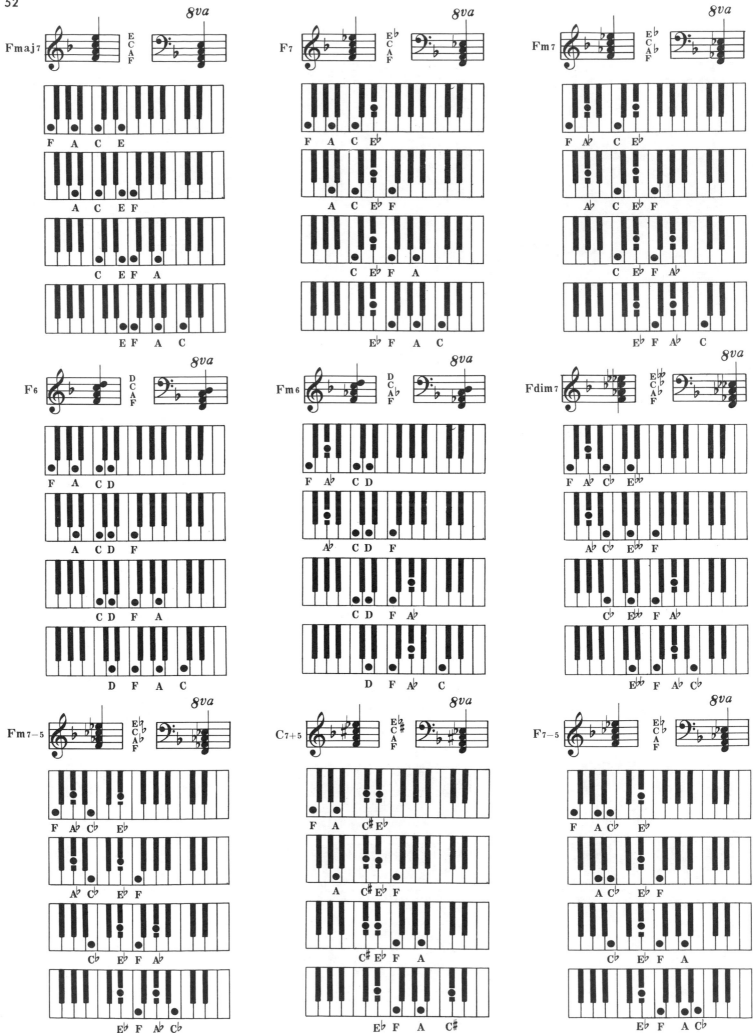

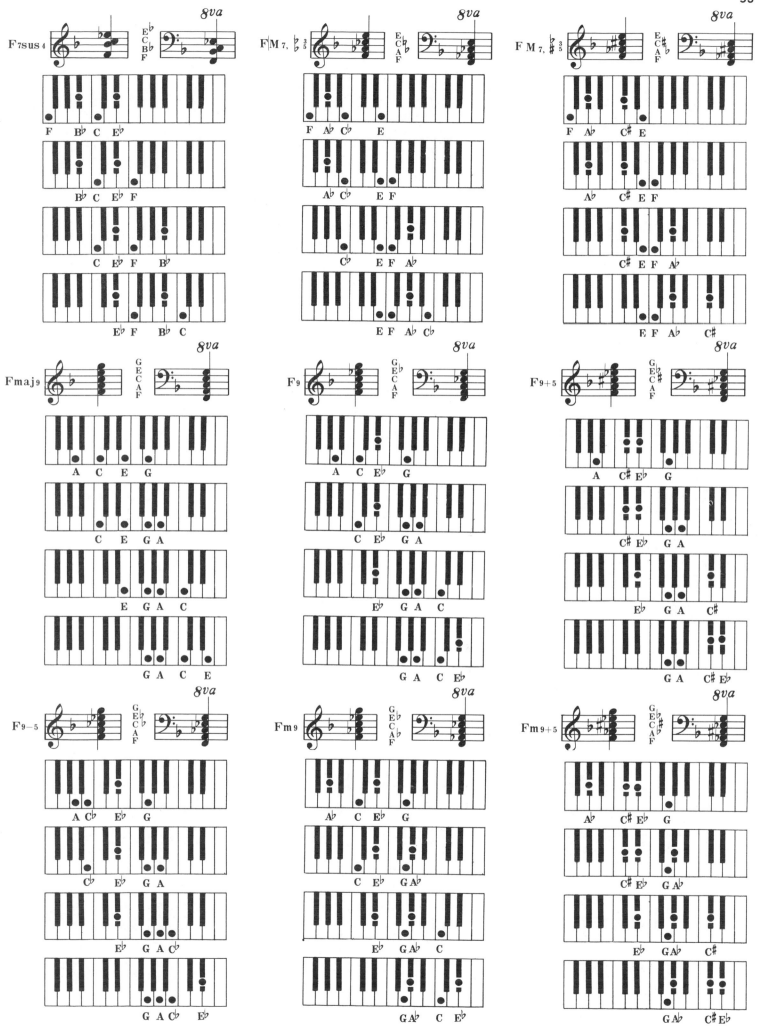

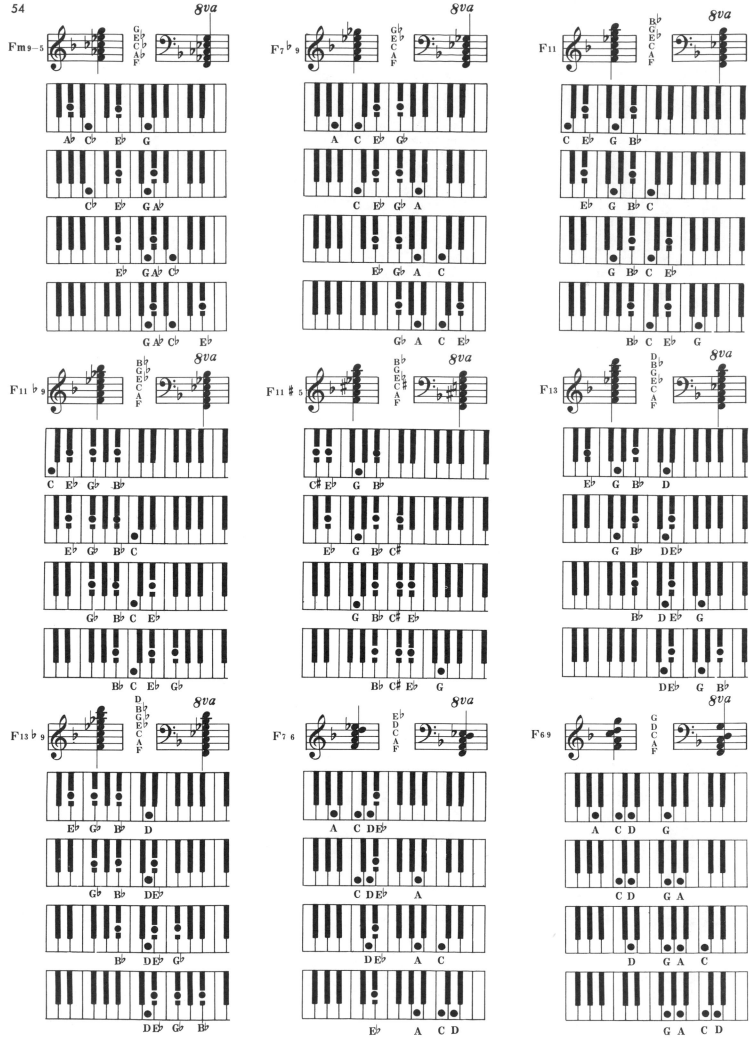

Key of F♯ Major (identical to G♭ Major)

F♯ Major Scale in One Octave

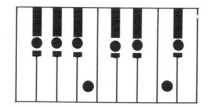

Scale Tones = F♯ G♯ A♯ B C♯ D♯ E♯ F♯

Scale Degrees = 1 2 3 4 5 6 7 8

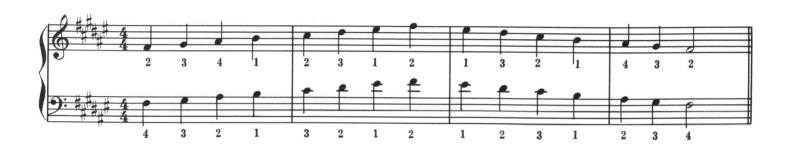

F♯ Major Scale in Two Octaves

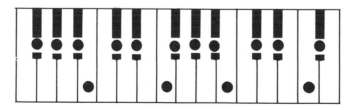

Scale Tones = F♯ G♯ A♯ B C♯ D♯ E♯ F♯ G♯ A♯ B C♯ D♯ E♯ F♯

Scale Degrees = 1 2 3 4 5 6 7 8 9 10 11 12 13 14 15

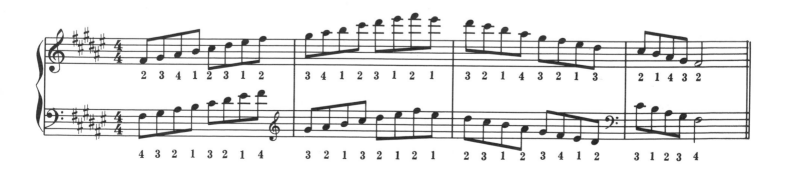

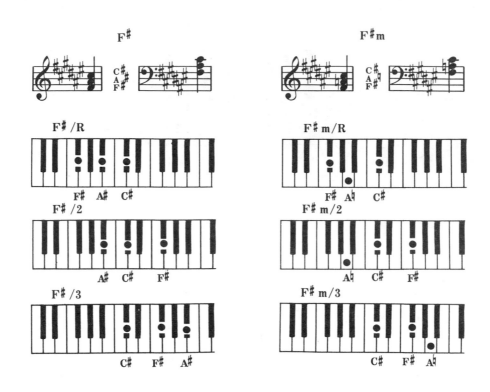

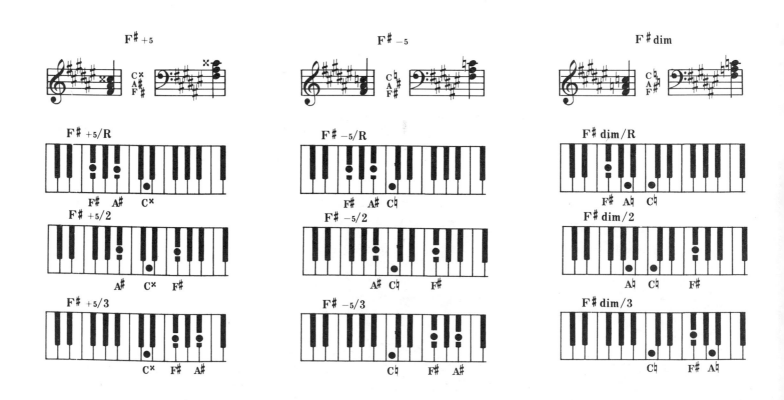

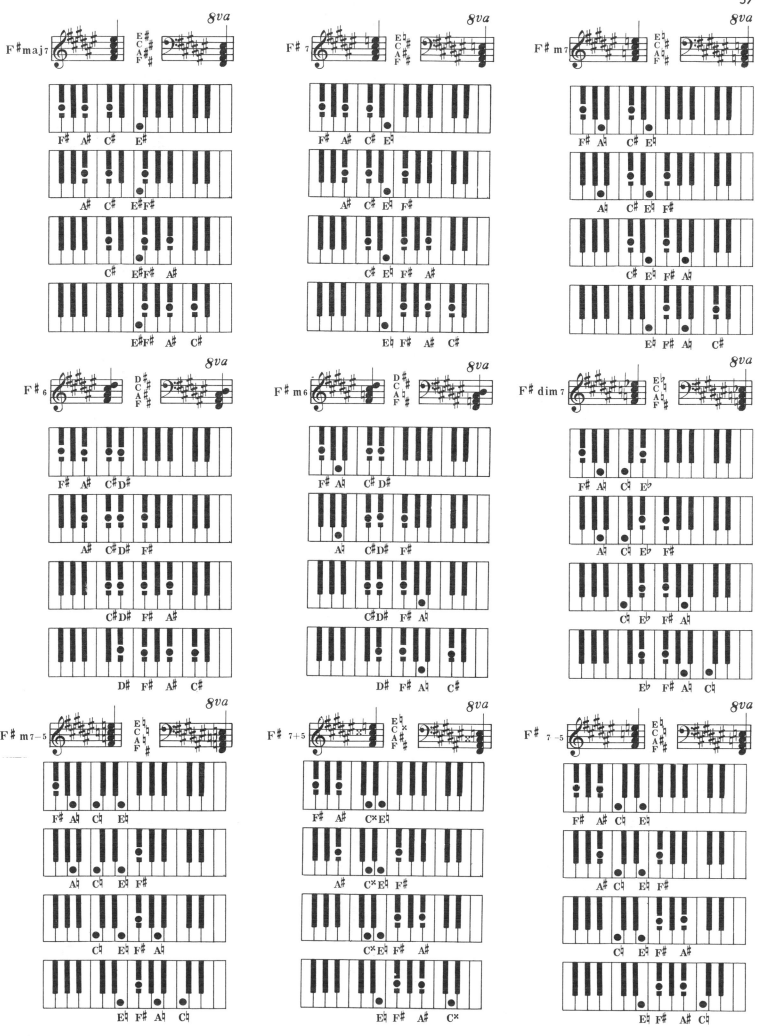

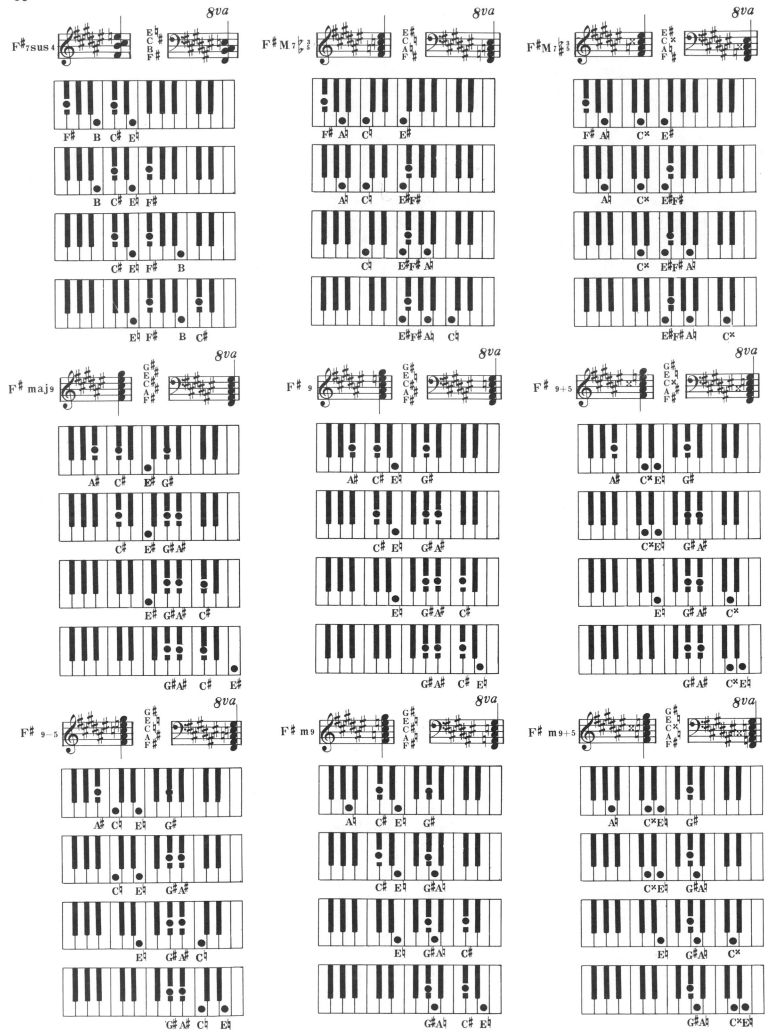

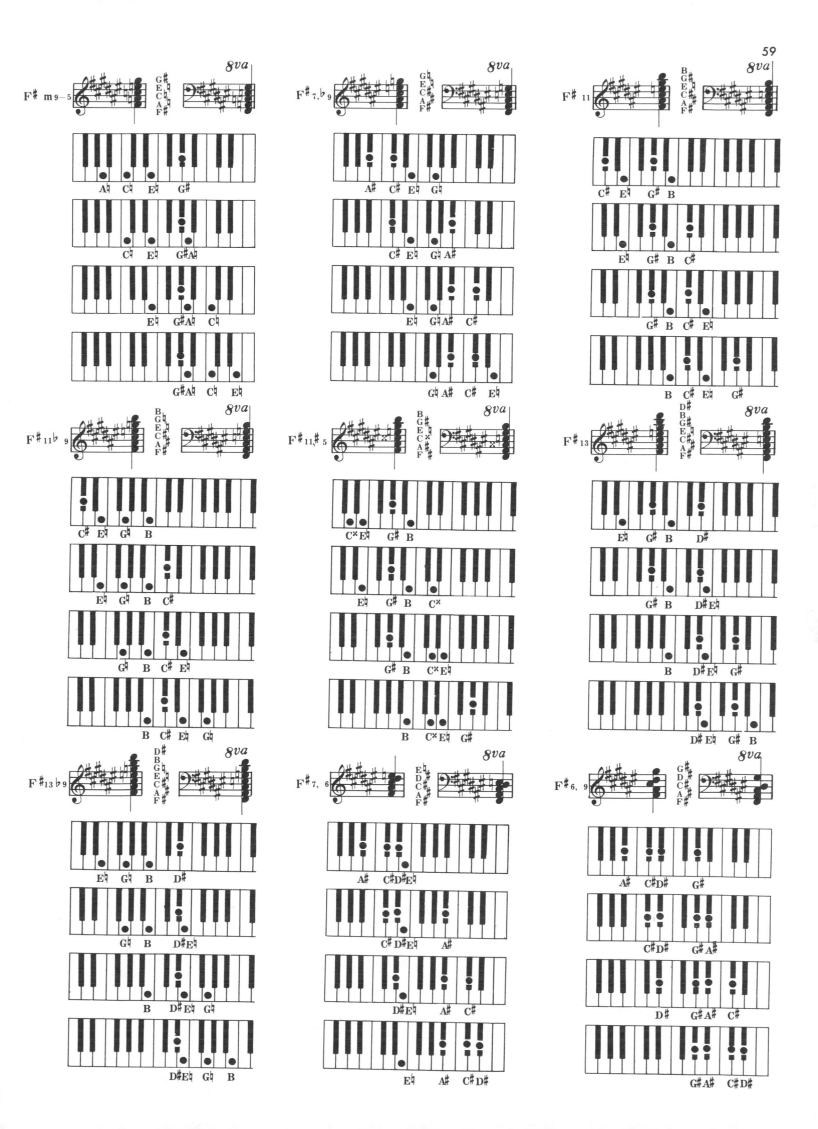

Key of G Major

G Major Scale in One Octave

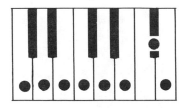

Scale Tones = G A B C D E F♯ G

Scale Degrees = 1 2 3 4 5 6 7 8

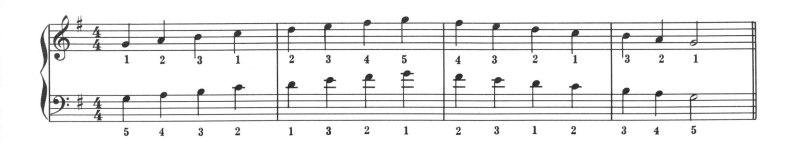

G Major Scale in Two Octaves

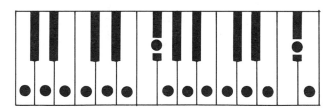

Scale Tones = G A B C D E F♯ G A B C D E F♯ G

Scale Degrees = 1 2 3 4 5 6 7 8 9 10 11 12 13 14 15

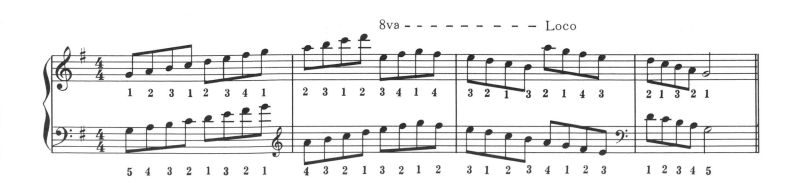

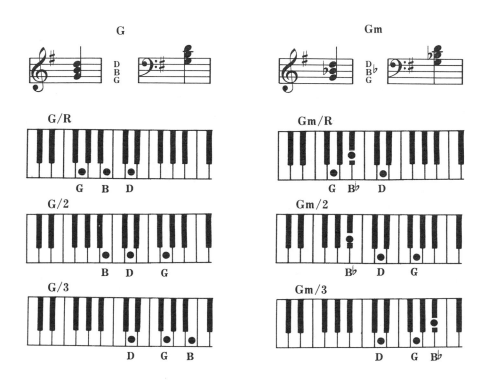

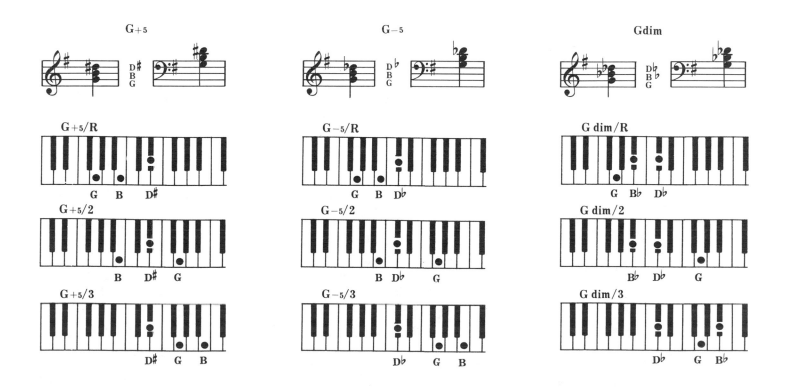

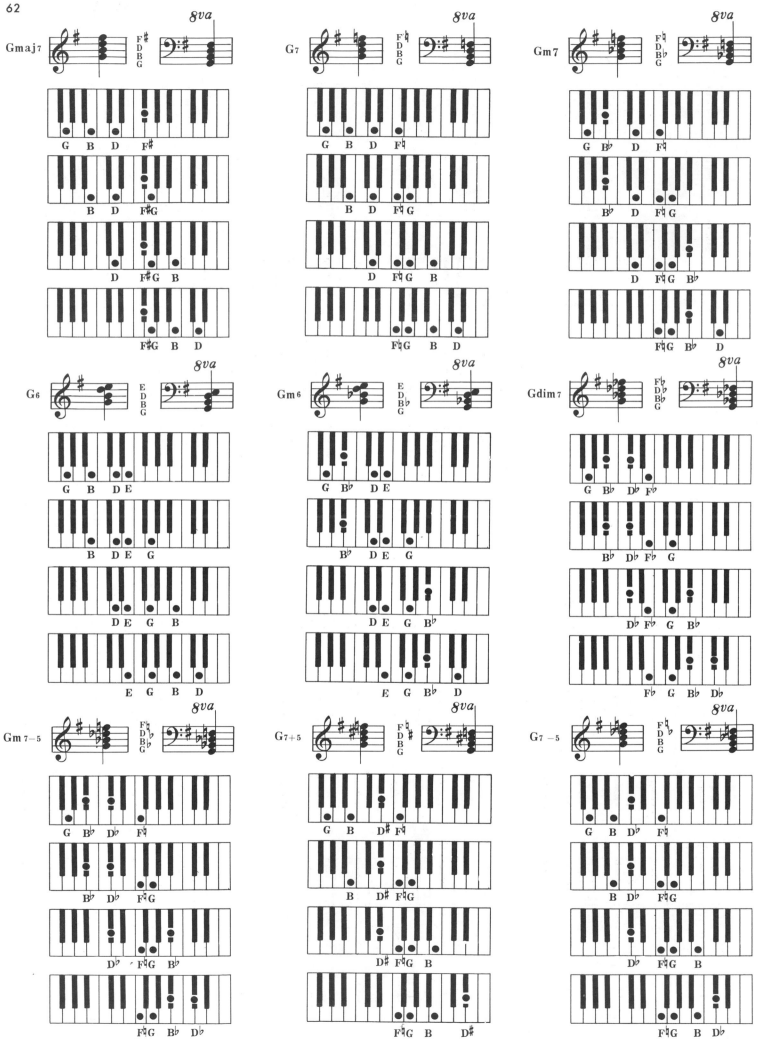

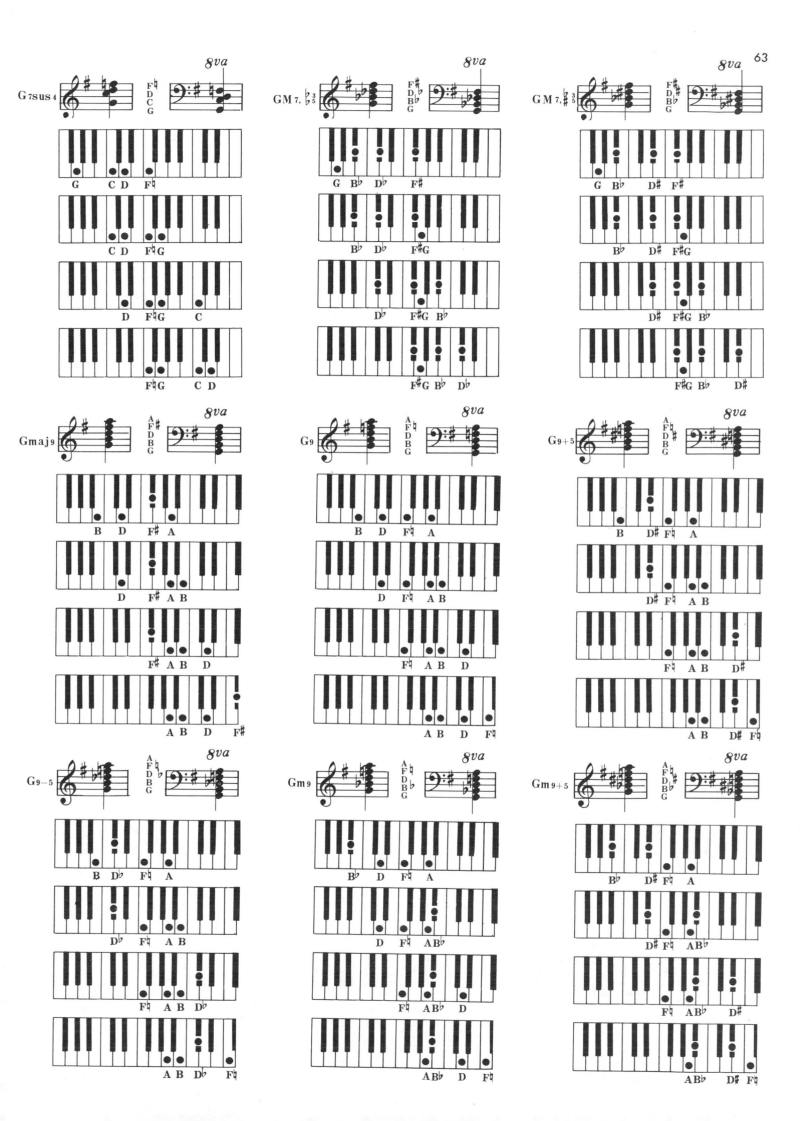

64

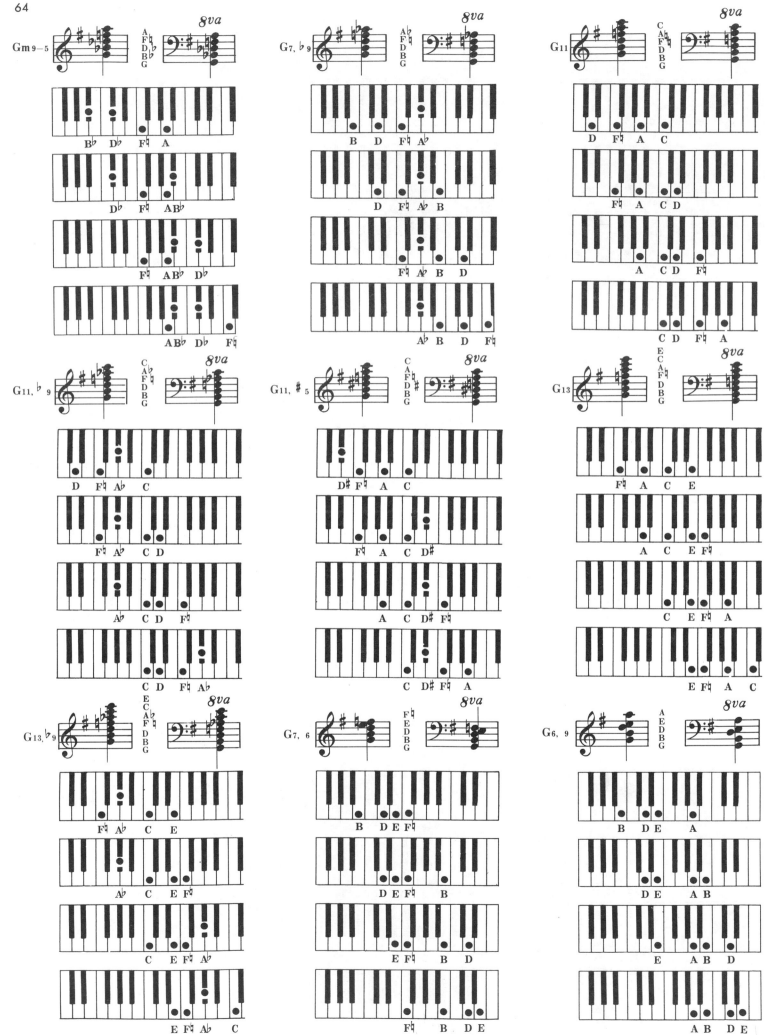#

Key of A♭ Major

A♭ Major Scale in One Octave

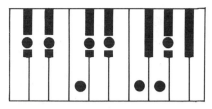

Scale Tones = A♭ B♭   C D♭ E♭ F G A♭

Scale Degrees = 1 2   3 4 5 6 7 8

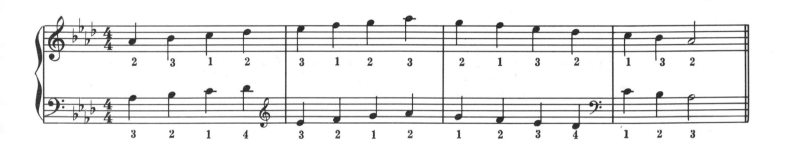

A♭ Major Scale in Two Octaves

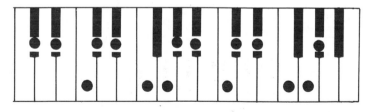

Scale Tones = A♭ B♭   C D♭ E♭ F G A♭ B♭ C D♭ E♭ F G A♭

Scale Degrees = 1 2   3 4 5 6 7 8 9 10 11 12 13 14 15

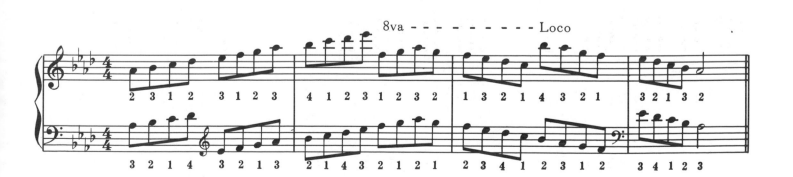

66

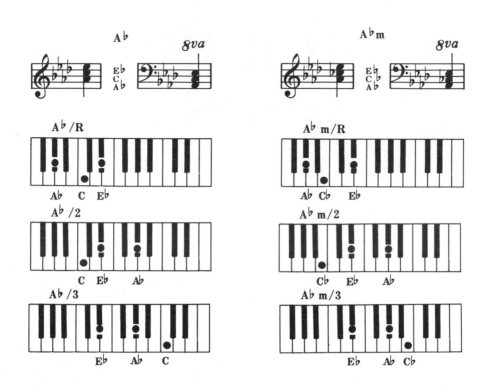

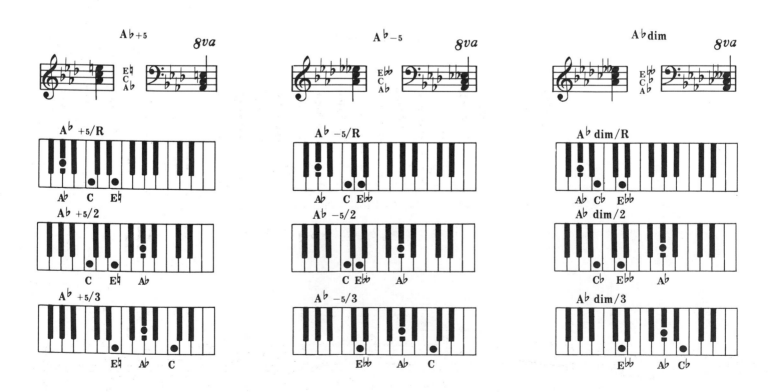

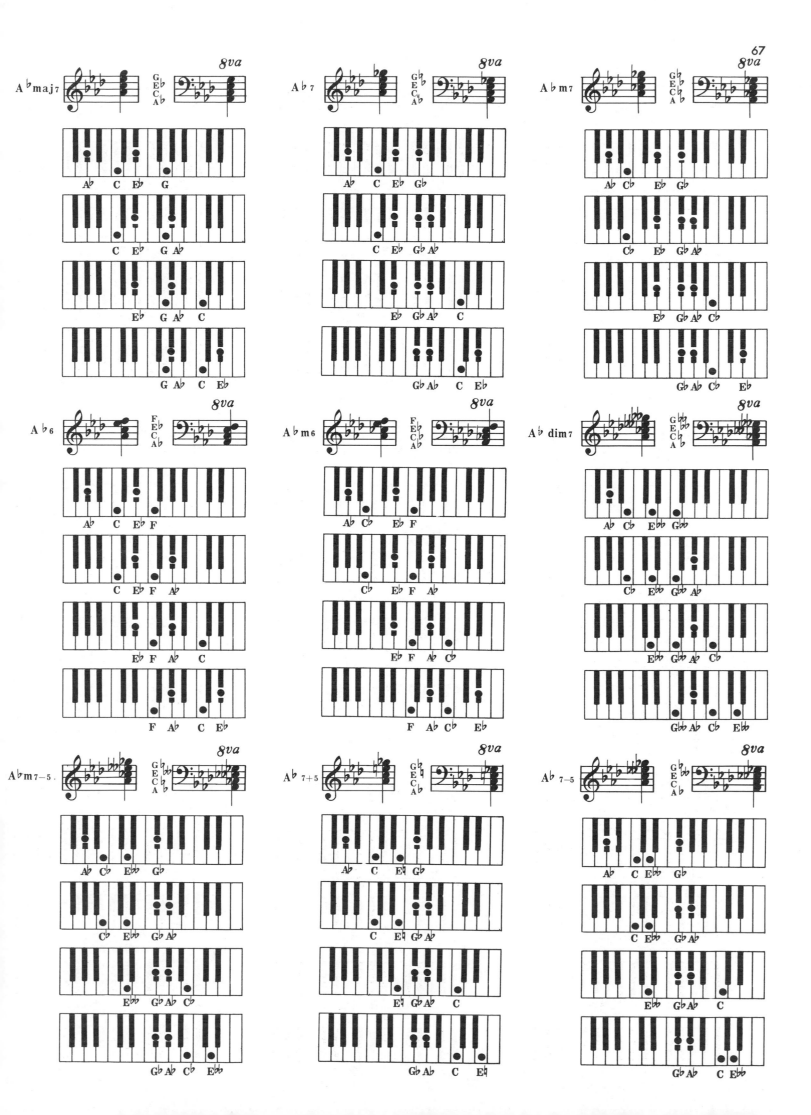

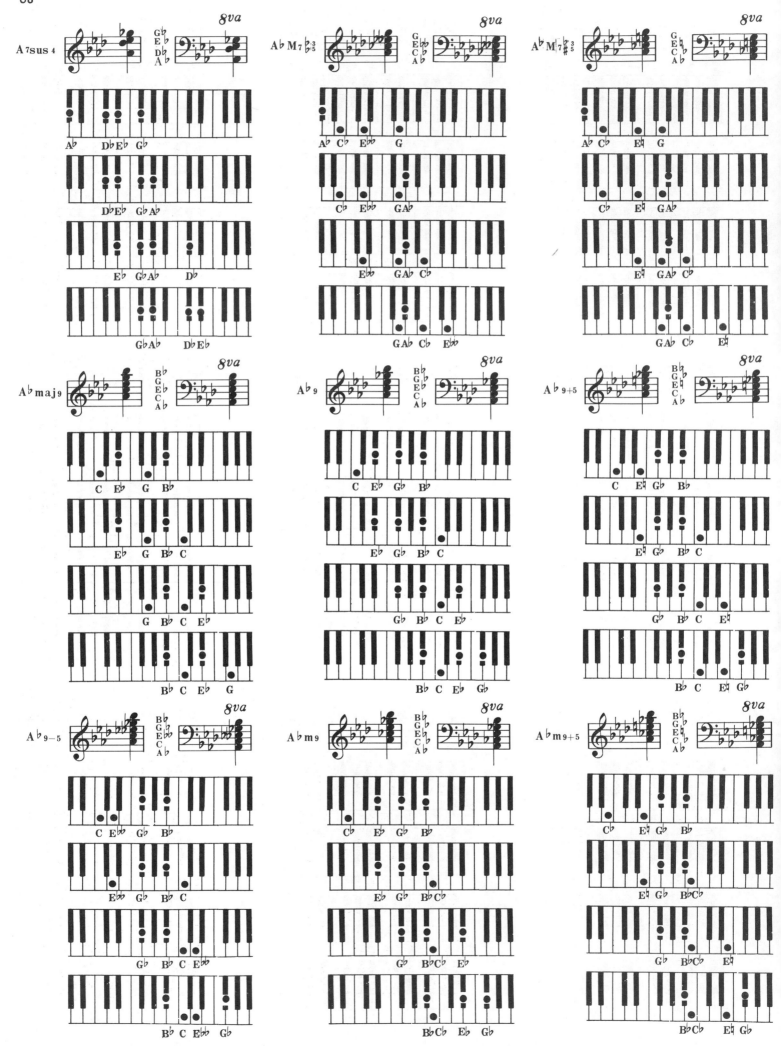

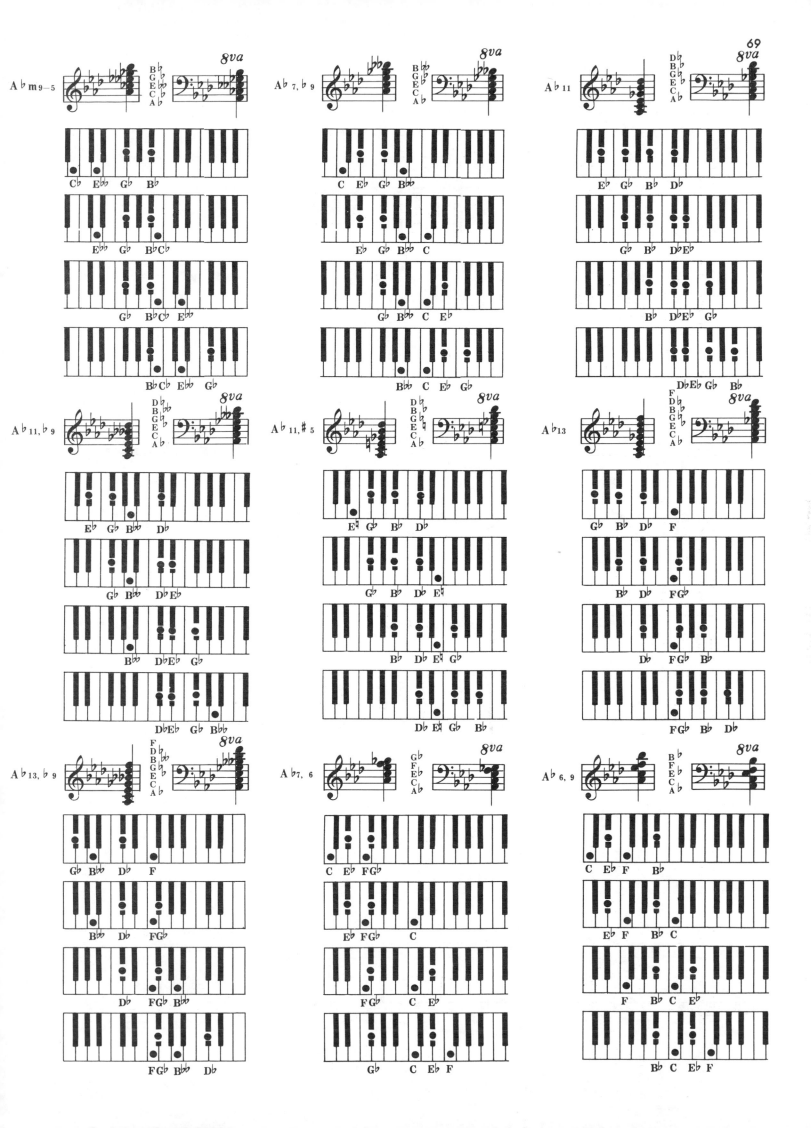

A Major Scale in One Octave

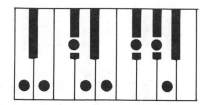

Scale Tones = A B C♯ D E F♯ G♯ A

Scale Degrees = 1 2 3 4 5 6 7 8

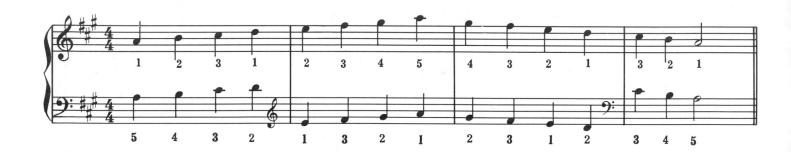

A Major Scale in Two Octaves

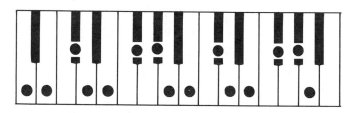

Scale Tones = A B C♯ D E F♯ G♯ A B C♯ D E F♯ G♯ A

Scale Degrees = 1 2 3 4 5 6 7 8 9 10 11 12 13 14 15

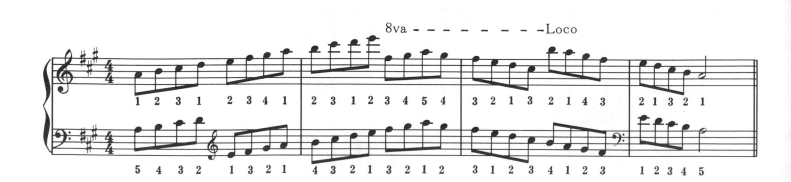

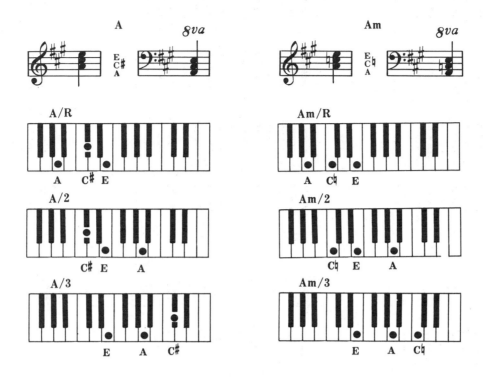

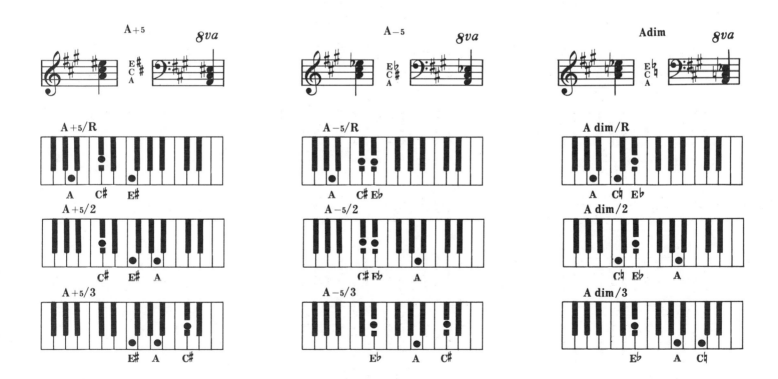

Amaj7 — A C# E G#

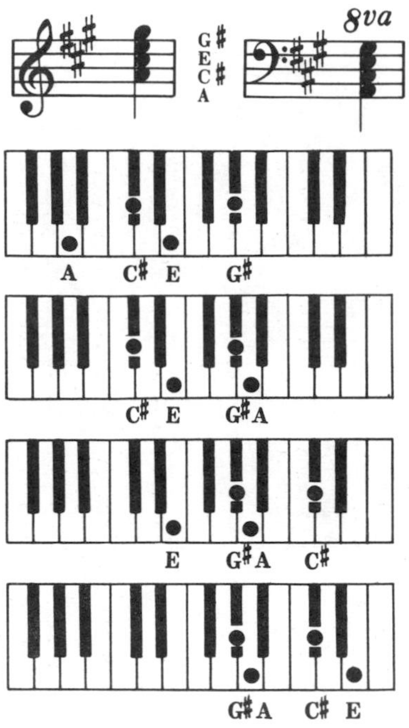

A7 — A C# E G♮

Am7 — A C♮ E G♮

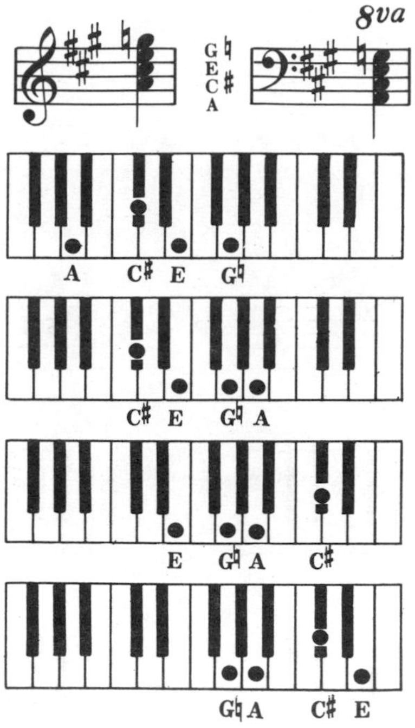

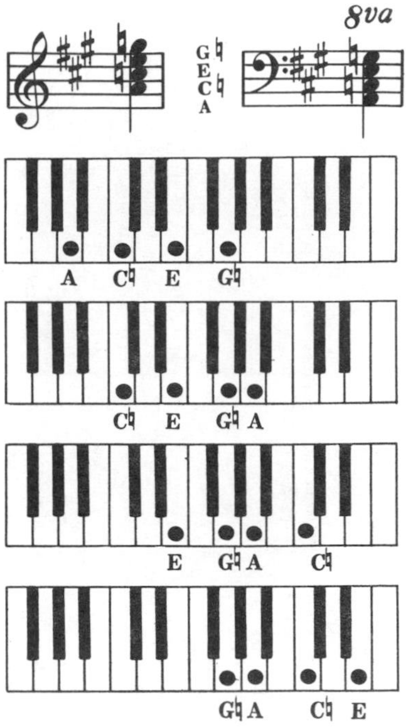

A6 — A C# E F#

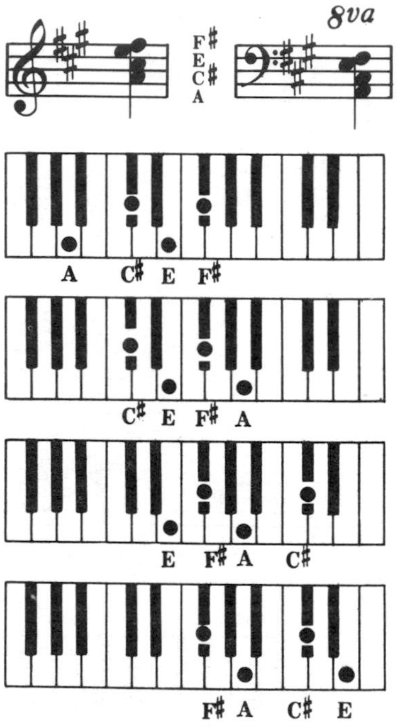

Am6 — A C♮ E F#

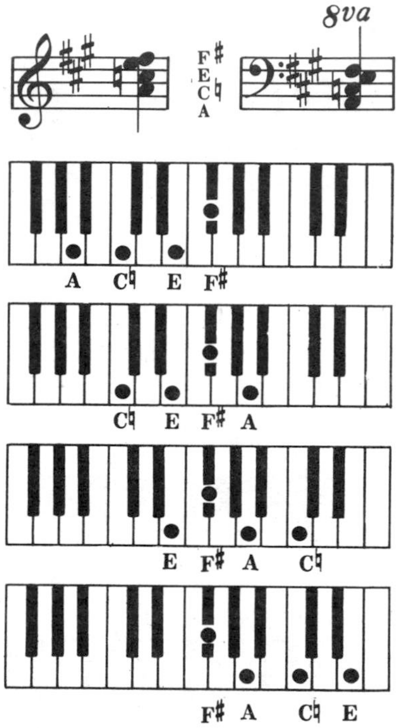

Adim7 — A C♮ E♭ G♭

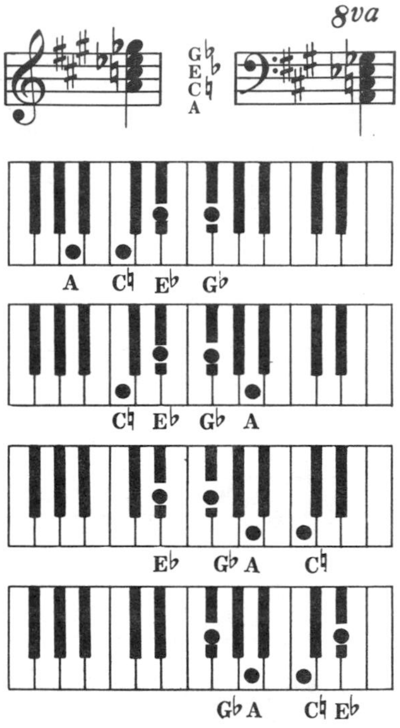

Am7-5 — A C♮ E♭ G♮

A7+5 — A C# E# G♮

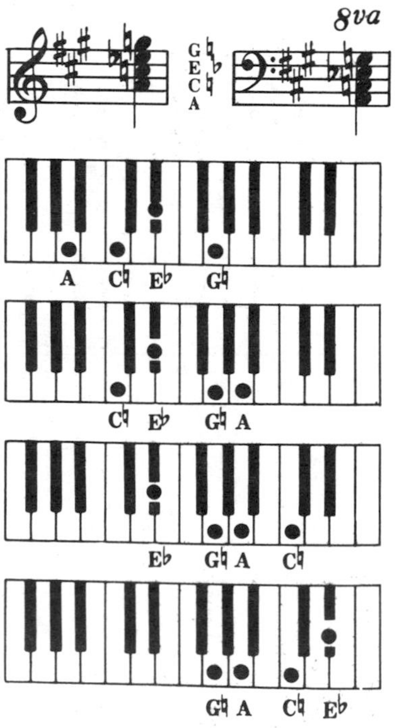

A7-5 — A C# E♭ G♮

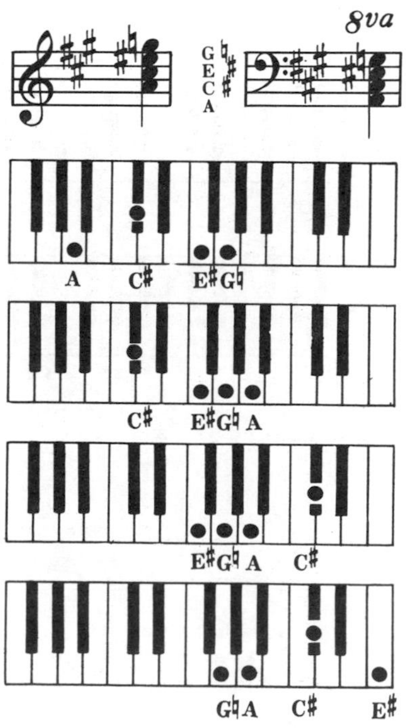

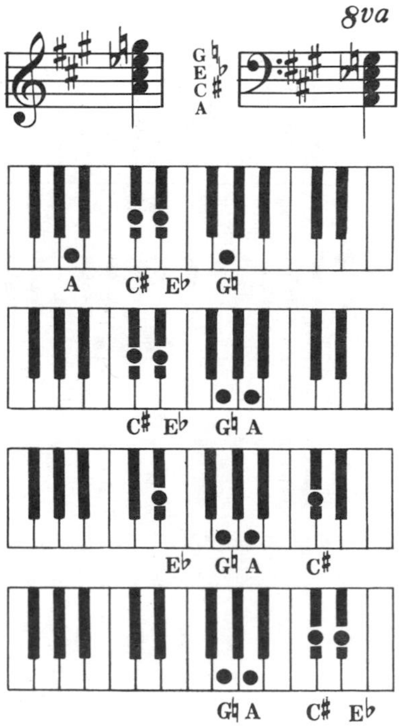

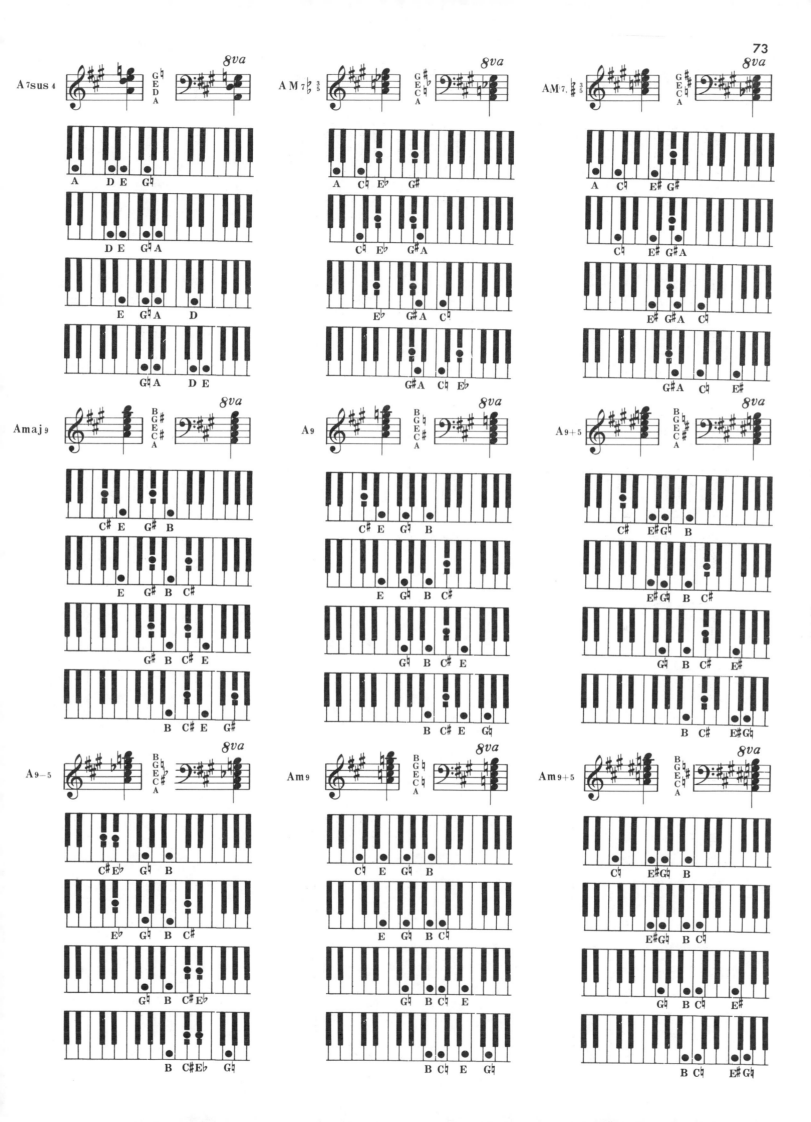

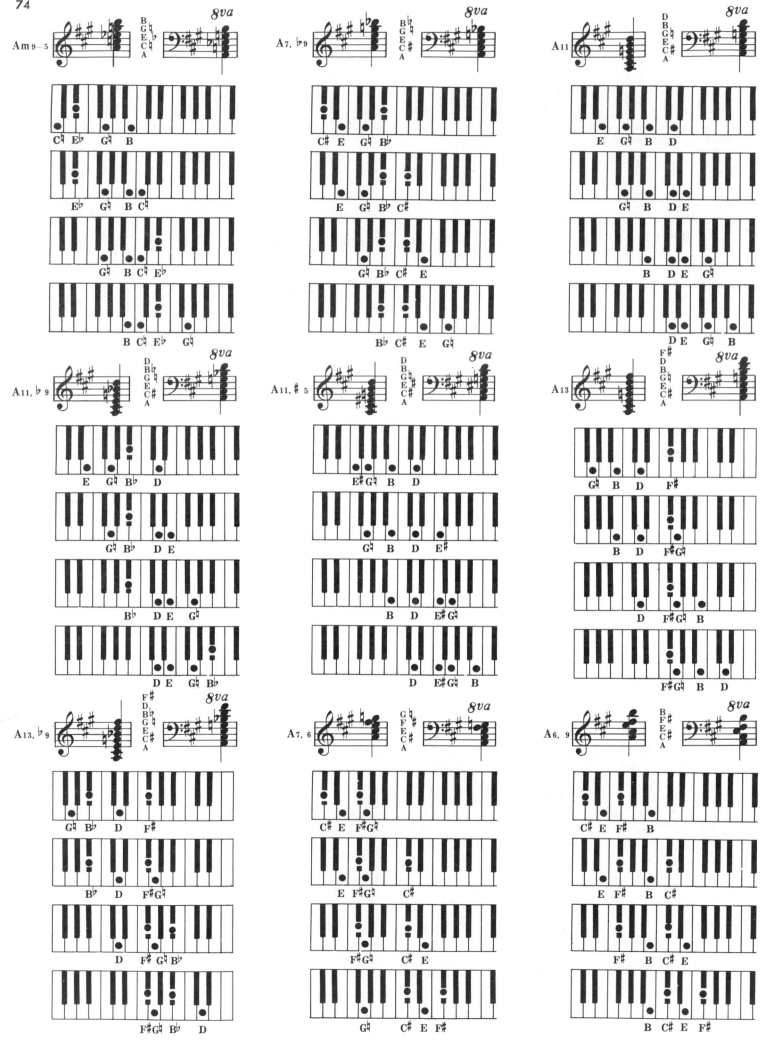

Key of B♭ Major

B♭ Major Scale in One Octave

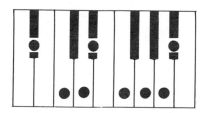

Scale Tones =	B♭		C	D	E♭		F	G	A	B♭
Scale Degrees =	1		2	3	4		5	6	7	8

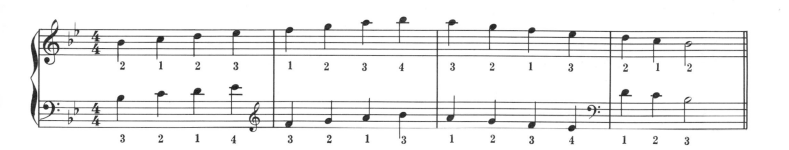

B♭ Major Scale in Two Octaves

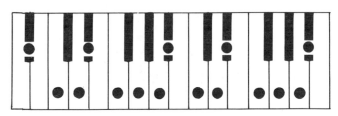

Scale Tones =	B♭	C	D	E♭	F	G	A	B♭	C	D	E♭	F	G	A	B♭
Scale Degrees =	1	2	3	4	5	6	7	8	9	10	11	12	13	14	15

8va - - - - - - - - Loco

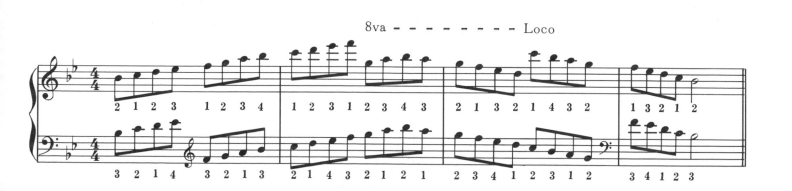

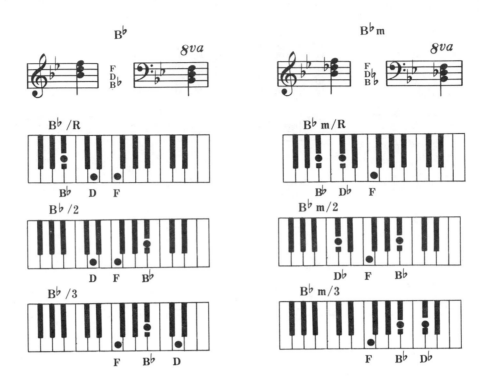

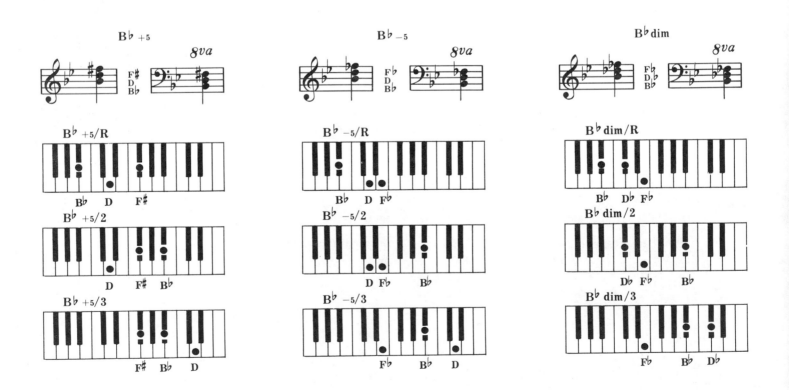

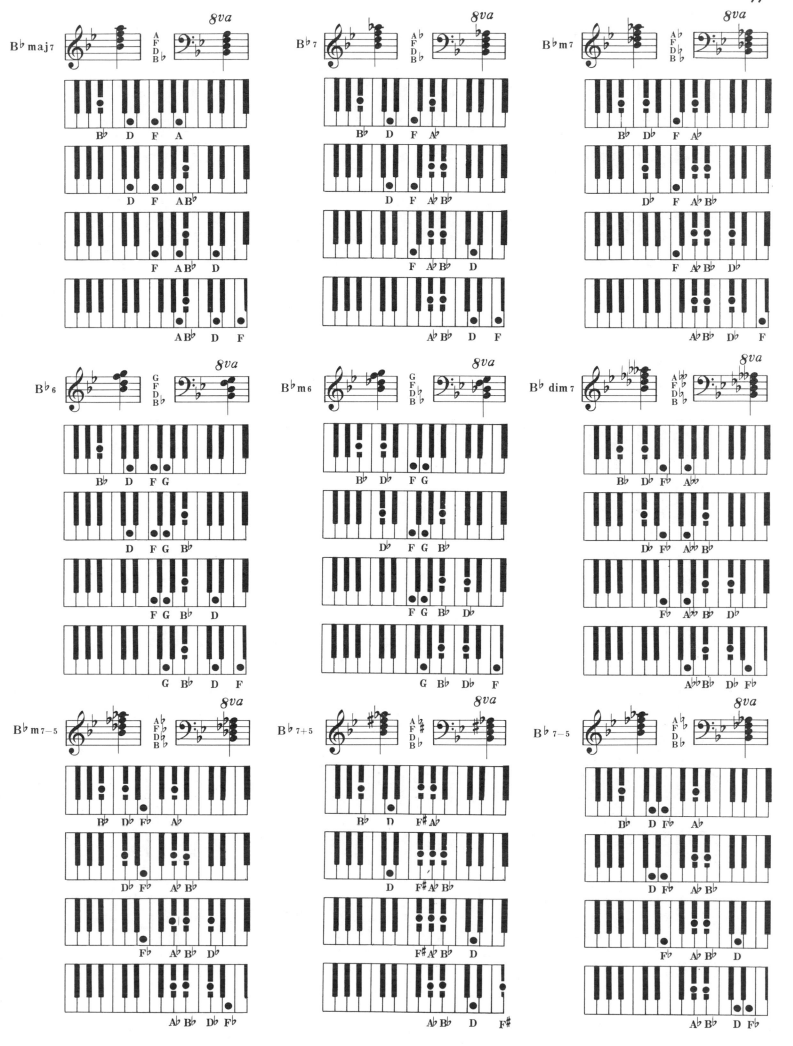

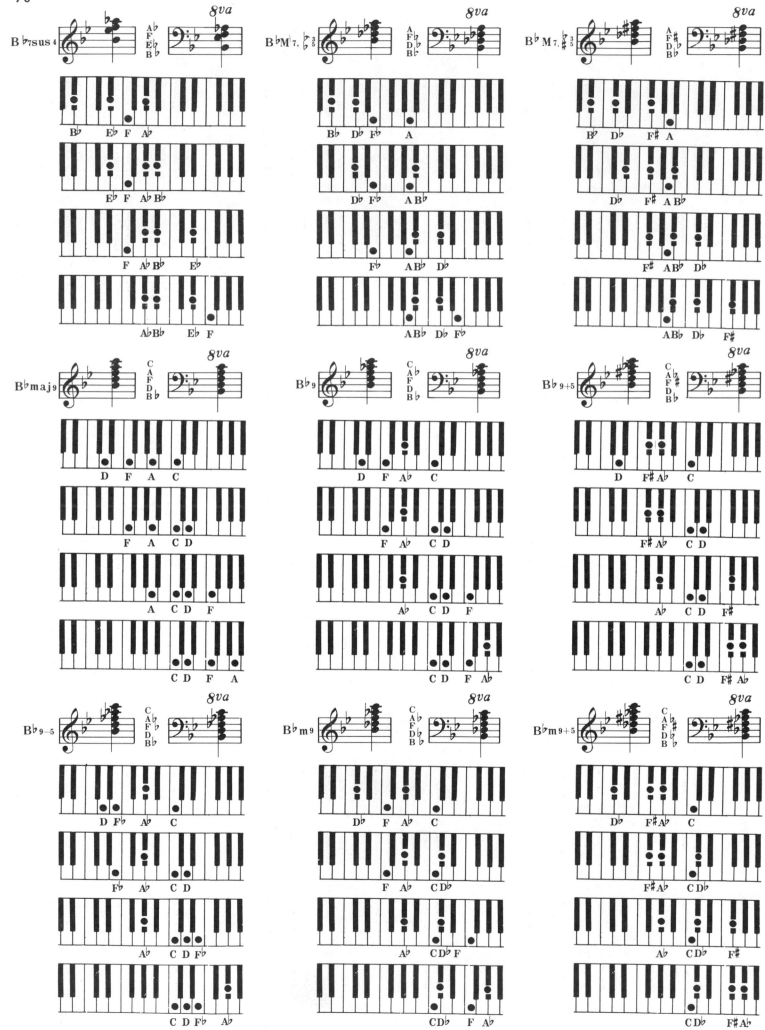

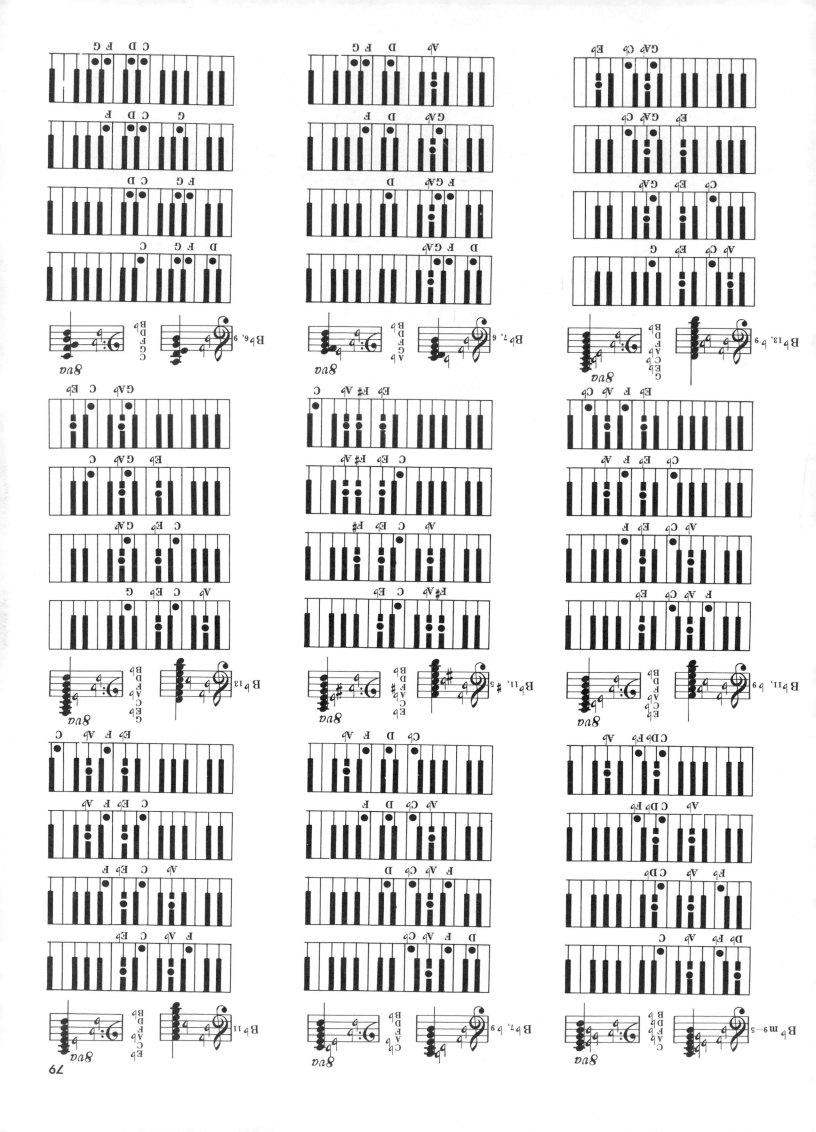

Key of B Major (identical to C♭)

B Major Scale in One Octave

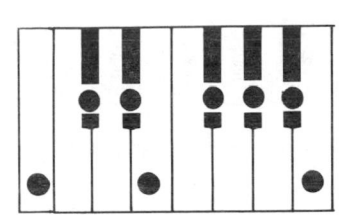

Scale Tones = B C♯ D♯ E   F♯ G♯ A♯ B
Scale Degrees = 1 2 3 4   5 6 7 8

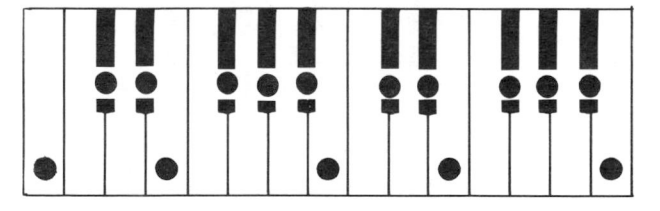

B Major Scale in Two Octaves

Scale Tones = B   C♯ D♯ E   F♯ G♯ A♯ B   C♯ D♯ E   F♯ G♯ A♯ B
Scale Degrees = 1   2 3 4   5 6 7   8   9 10 11   12 13 14 15

8va - - - - - - - - Loco

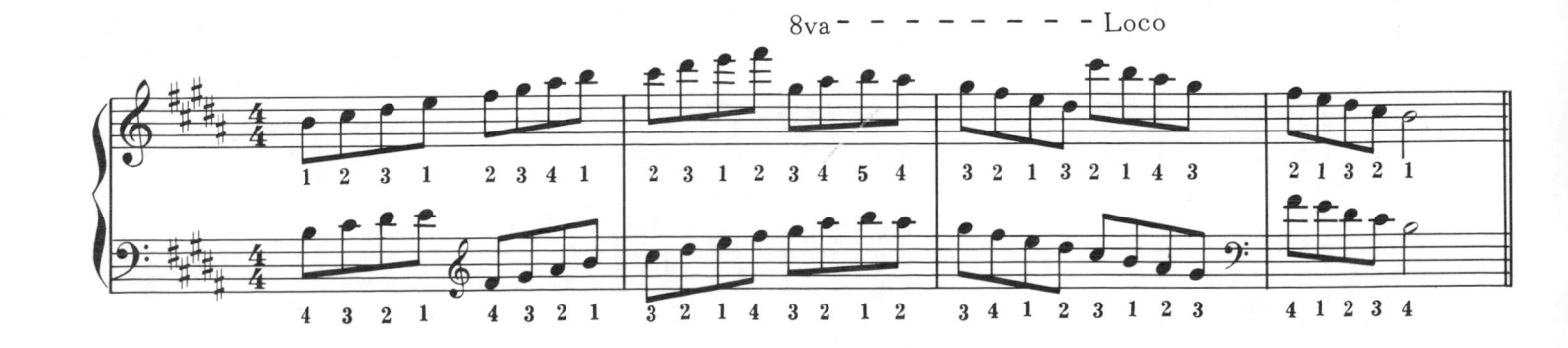

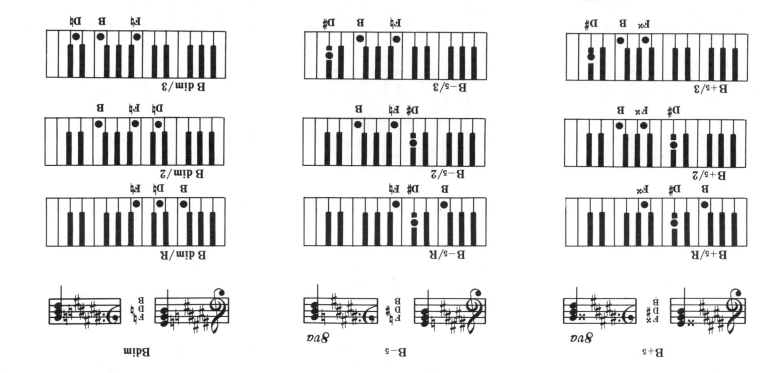

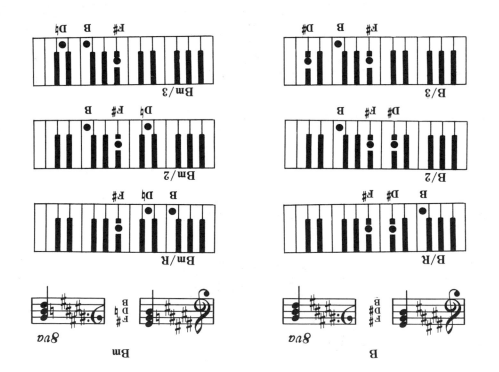

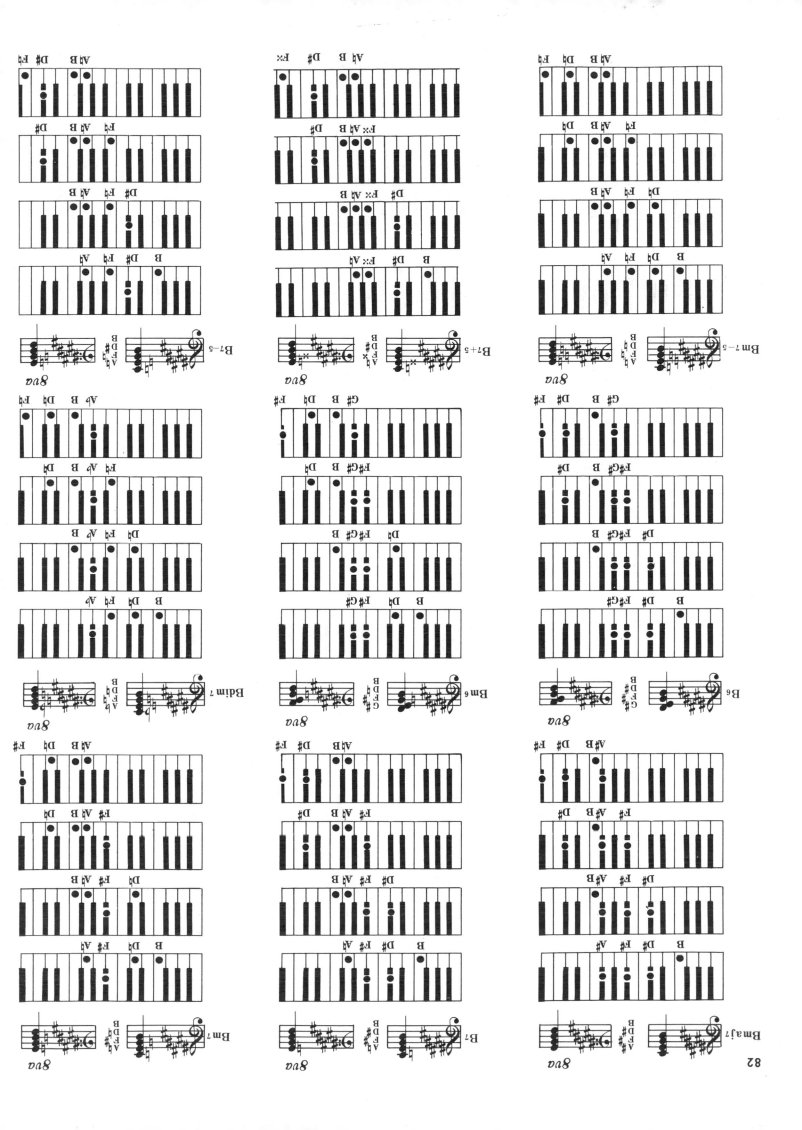

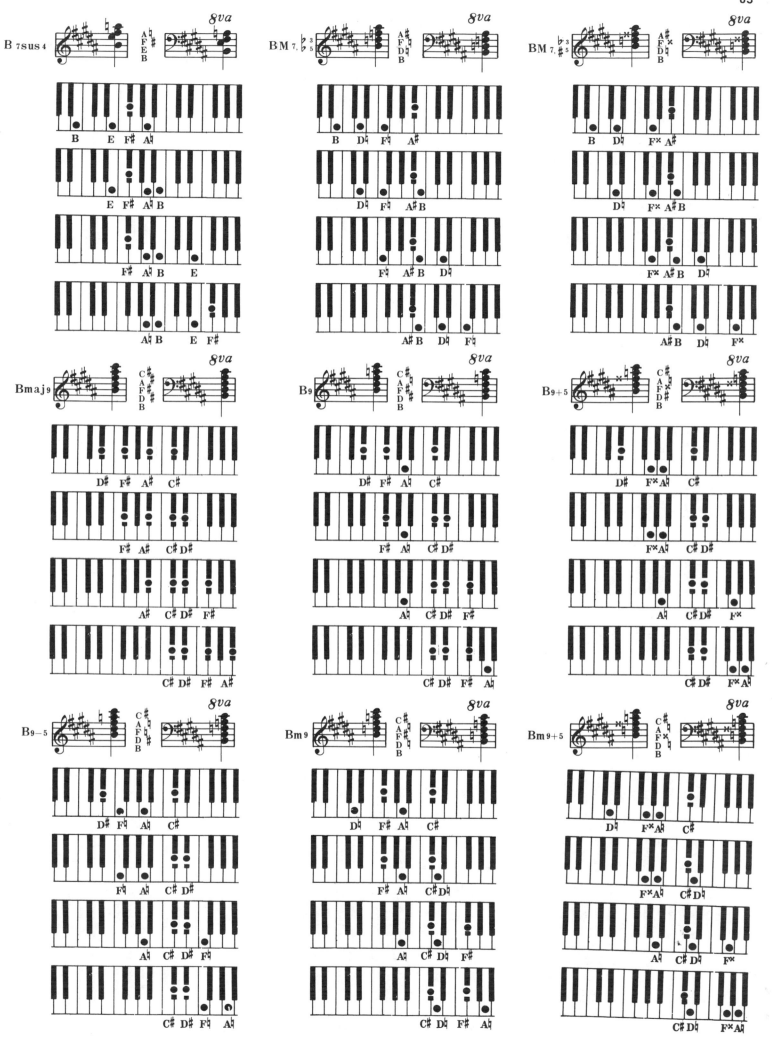

83

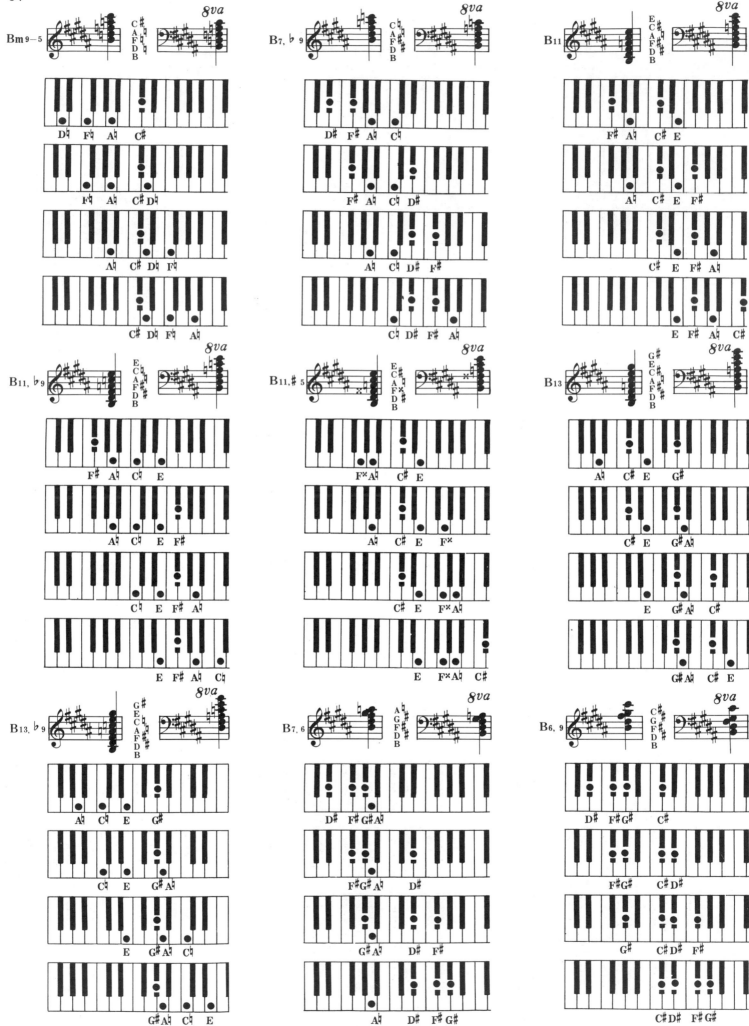

Range of the Bass, Chords and Melody

Here is a keyboard diagram showing the ranges used for the bass, chords and melodies of popular songs:

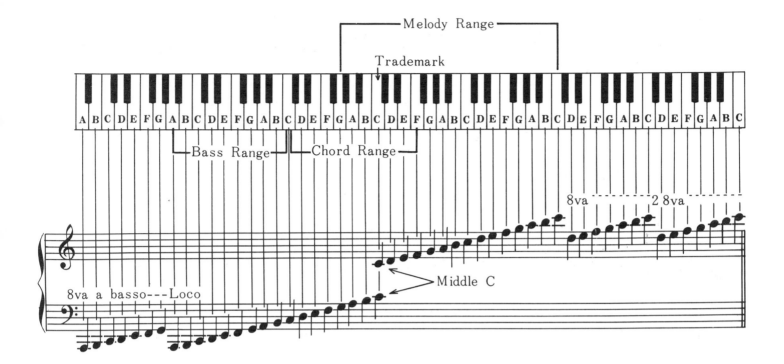

Here is a chart showing the bass and chords in root position for the C, Dm, F, and G chords which will be used in the examples on the following pages:

C

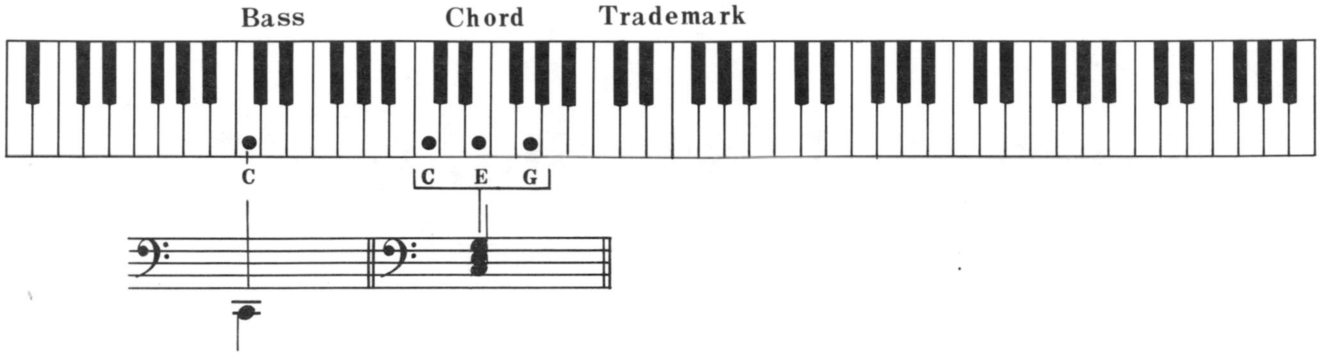

Bass   Chord   Trademark

Dm

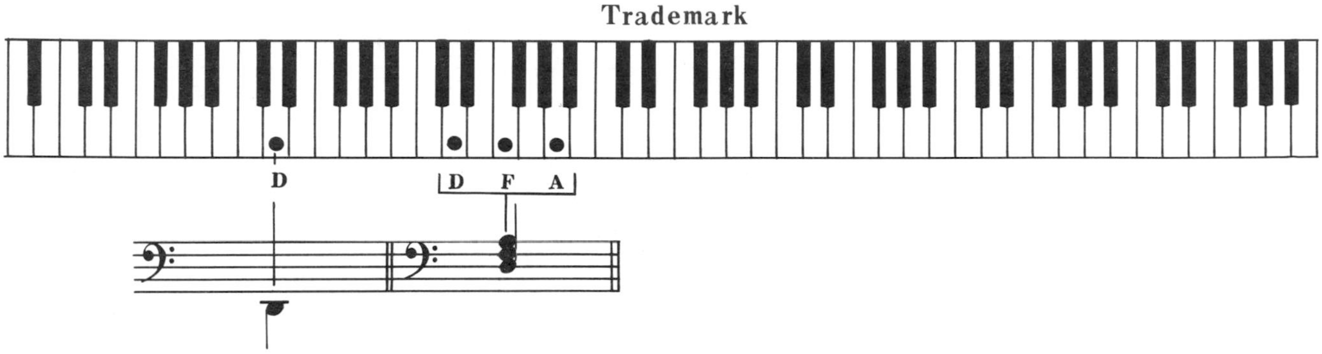

Trademark

F

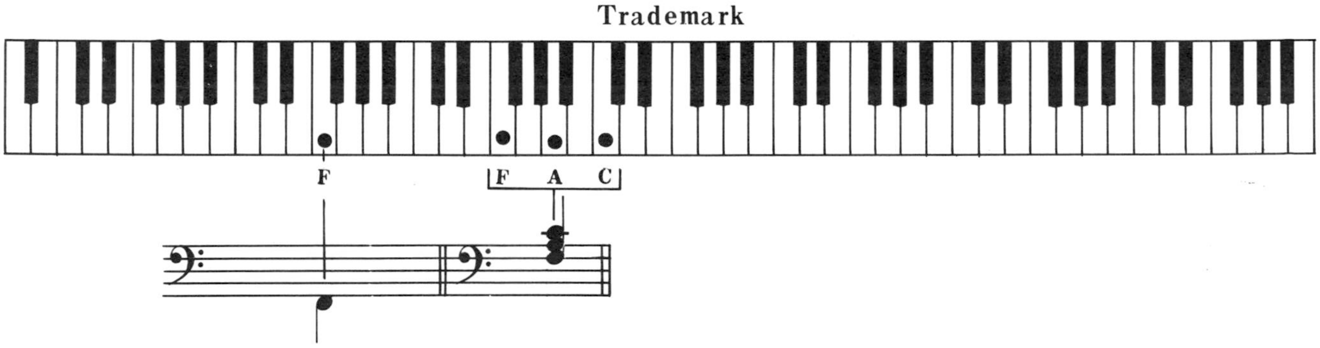

Trademark

G

Trademark

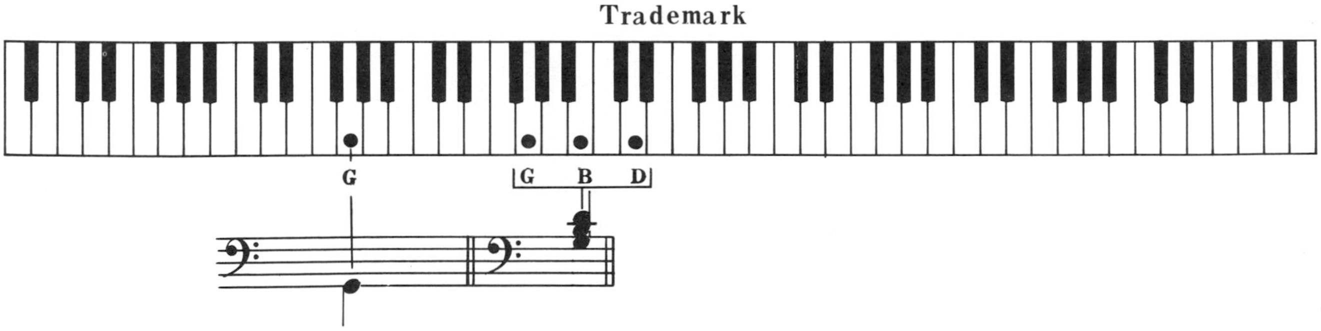

Using Chords To Play Popular Songs

Many popular songs are written in **lead sheet form** showing only the chords, melody and lyrics:

The simplest method of interpreting the lead sheet is to play the melody with the right hand and to play sustained chords with the left hand.

The time signature $\frac{3}{4}$ means that there are three counts in each measure. The left hand plays the chord at the beginning of each measure and sustains the chord for all three counts:

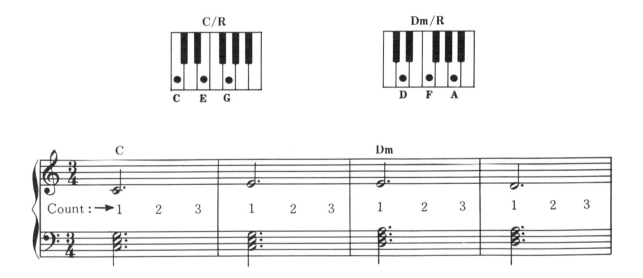

The keyboard diagrams shown above each song in this book are to help the student learn the chords and to see how they are used.

Notice that one chord per measure has been used, each chord being repeated in succesive measures until the chord symbol changes.

Root position chords are being used because they are easily remembered.

Here is the entire song which was presented as an example on the previous page.

Play this selection with sustained chords.

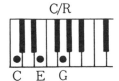

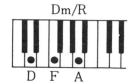

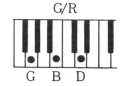

When I Hold You

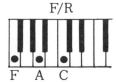

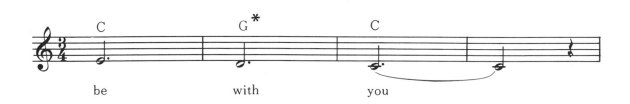

*NOTE: omit the note D in the G major triad in the left hand when it conflicts with the D in the melody in the right hand.

The Waltz Rhythm Pattern

The waltz rhythm pattern is found in the time signature of $\frac{3}{4}$, this means that there are three counts in each measure.

The waltz rhythm pattern is counted. 1.   2.   3.
"One" "Two" "Three"

The waltz rhythm pattern is played : Bass   Chord Chord
(Abbreviated   : B   C   C   )

The "Bass" is the root of the chord played an octave lower than the "Chord."

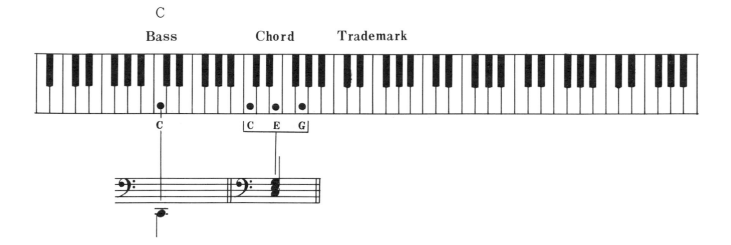

Left hand alone:

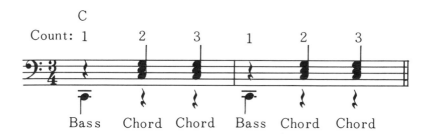

Right hand plays the melody while
Left hand plays the waltz rhythm pattern:

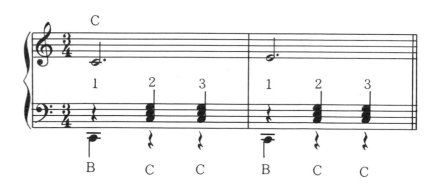

Coordination Exercise: Waltz #1.

Coordination exercises are designed to give the student an opportunity to practice coordinating rhythm patterns with simple melodies and chords.

In this coordination exercise the waltz rhythm pattern is abbreviated and placed below the count to help visualize the coordination of the melody and rhythm pattern.

C/R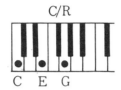
C E G

Dm/R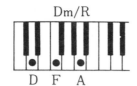
D F A

F/R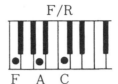
F A C

G/R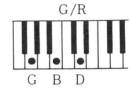
G B D

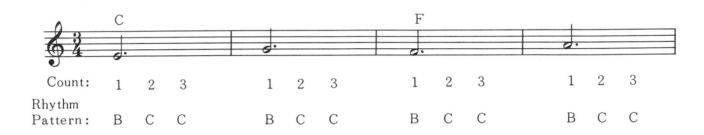

Count: 1 2 3   1 2 3   1 2 3   1 2 3

Rhythm
Pattern: B C C   B C C   B C C   B C C

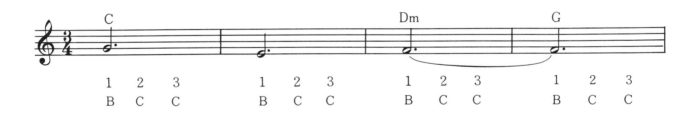

1 2 3   1 2 3   1 2 3   1 2 3
B C C   B C C   B C C   B C C

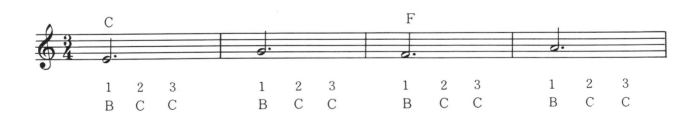

1 2 3   1 2 3   1 2 3   1 2 3
B C C   B C C   B C C   B C C

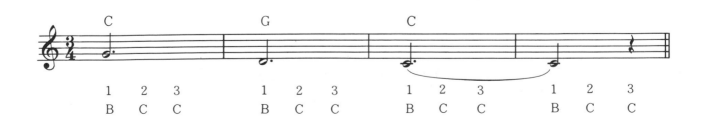

1 2 3   1 2 3   1 2 3   1 2 3
B C C   B C C   B C C   B C C

The Fox Trot Rhythm Pattern

The fox trot rhythm pattern is found in the time signature of $\frac{4}{4}$, sometimes written C (which means common time). This means that there are four counts per measure.

The fox trot rhythm pattern is counted :

	1.	2.	3.	4.
	"One"	"Two"	"Three"	"Four"
The fox trot rhythm pattern is played :	Bass	Chord	Bass	Chord
(Abbreviated :	B	C	B	C)

The "Bass" is the root of the chord and is played an octave lower the "Chord."

C

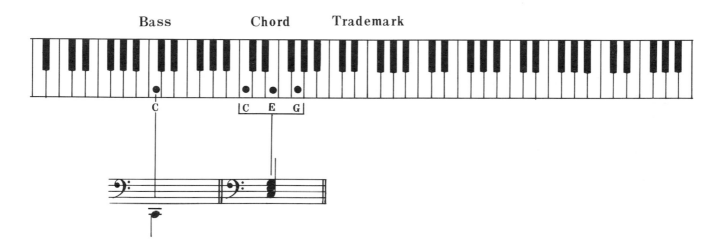

Left hand alone:

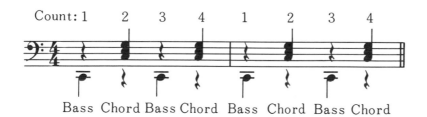

Right hand plays the melody while
Left hand plays the fox trot rhythm pattern:

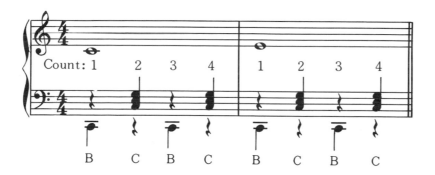

Coordination Exercise: Fox Trot #1.

In this exercise the fox trot rhtyhm pattern has been abbreviated and placed below the count in order to help visualize the coordination of the melody and the rhythm pattern.

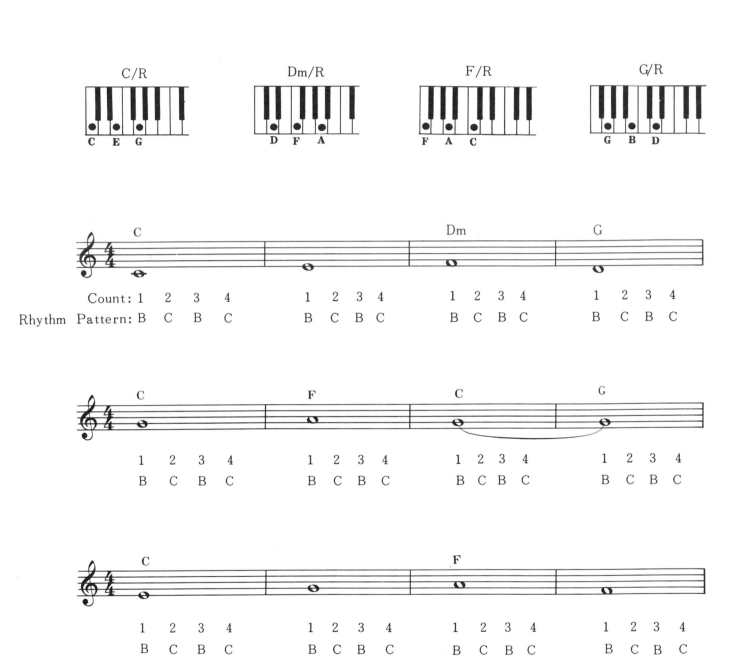

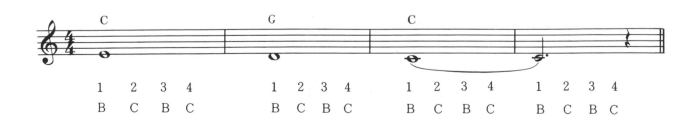

The fox trot rhythm pattern is also used for fast tempos such as polkas and marches.

The fox trot rhythm pattern is often written in $\frac{2}{4}$ metre, also written as. ¢

In $\frac{2}{4}$ metre the fox trot rhythm pattern is counted : 1.   +   2.   +
                          "One"   "And"   "Two"   "And"

In $\frac{2}{4}$ metre the fox trot rhythm pattern is played : Bass   Chord   Bass   Chord
                 (Abbreviated   : B   C   B   C   )

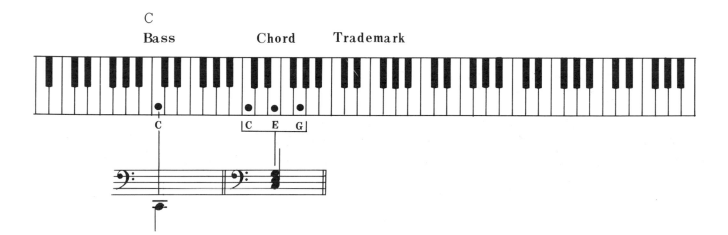

Left hand alone:

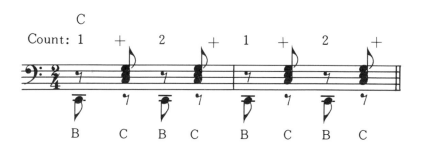

Right hand plays the melody while
the left hand plays the fox trot rhythm pattern:

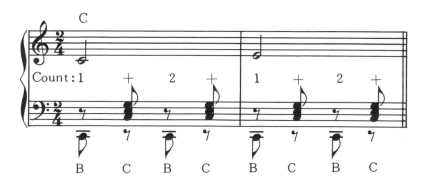

Alternating the Bass.

Repeating the same bass note creates a certain monotony called **the droning effect.**
To avoid the droning effect **alternate** the bass.

The following chart shows which chord-tones to use when alternating the bass:

Chord	Fundamental Bass	Alternating Bass
Major Chord	Root (R)	Fifth (5)
Minor Chord	Root (R)	Fifth (5)
Augmented Chord	Root (R)	Third (3)
Lowered Fifth Chord	Root (R)	Third (3)
Diminished Chord	Root (R)	Flatted Third (♭3)

Here are some examples of the alternating bass a for C major Triad:

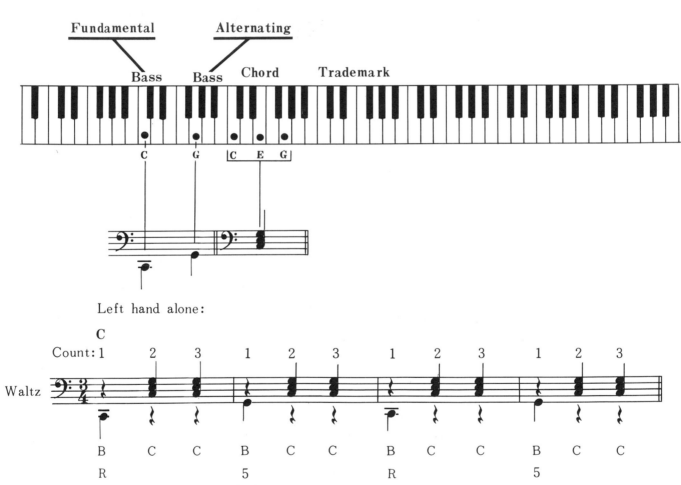

Left hand alone:

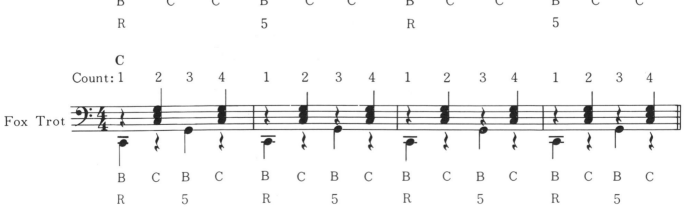

Using Different Chord Positions

When all of the chords in a song are played in root position the transitions between chords are not smoothe because of the necessary hand movement up and down the staff:

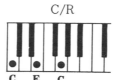

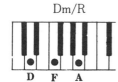

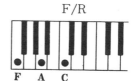

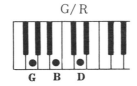

Smoother transitions between chords can be made by using different chord positions:

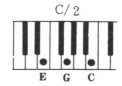

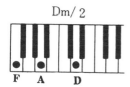

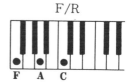

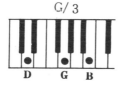

Alternating the Alternating Bass

Often in the transition between chords a droning effect occurs in the bass even though the bass is alternating:

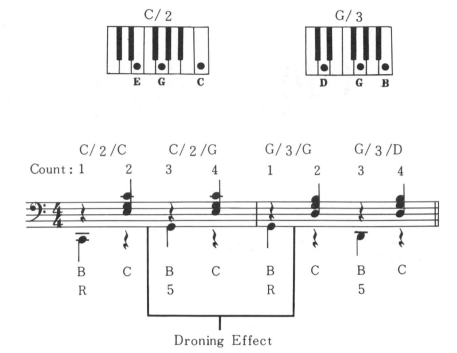

Notice that the alternating bass for both chords is root and fifth (R and 5). The droning effect is created because of the repetition of the G bass notes in the transition between the C and G chords, C/2/G and G/3/G

To avoid the droning effect simply alternate the alternating bass notes:

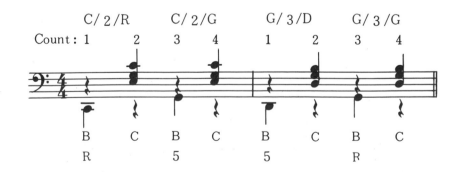

Reversing the order of the alternating bass notes in the G chord now avoids the droning efect:

C/2/G - G/3/D